How to Raise and Keep a Dragon

How to Raise and Keep a Dragon

by
JOHN TOPSELL

EXECUTIVE EDITOR JOSEPH NIGG
ILLUSTRATIONS DAN MALONE

APPLE

A QUARTO BOOK

First published in the UK in 2008 by
Apple Press
7 Greenland Street
London NW1 0ND
www.apple-press.com

Copyright © 2008 Quarto Publishing plc

ISBN: 978-1-84543-282-9

QUAR.RKP

Conceived, designed, and produced by
Quarto Publishing plc
The Old Brewery, 6 Blundell Street
London N7 9BH

Editors: Susie May,
Karen Koll
Art Editors: Anna Knight,
Natasha Montgomery
Assistant Art Director:
Penny Cobb
Copy Editor: Tracie Davis
Proofreader: Claire
Wedderburn
Maxwell
Indexer: Dorothy Frame
Designer: Karin Skånberg
Illustrator: Dan Malone

Art Director: Moira Clinch
Publisher: Paul Carslake

Manufactured by Modern Age Repro House
Ltd, Hong Kong
Printed by Midas Printing International
limited, China

9 8 7 6 5 4 3 2 1

Asian Dragon page 24

Contents

Cockatrice page 26

Dragon of India page 28

Drakon page 30

part 3
Raising the Perfect Dragon page 52

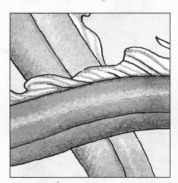

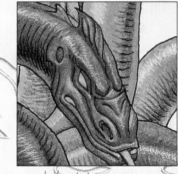

Joppa Dragon page 32

Multiheaded Dragon page 34

Mushussu page 36

Piasa page 38

Rainbow Serpent page 40

part 4
Training Your Dragon page 90

part 5
Presenting Your Dragon page 108

Salamander page 42

Sea Dragon page 44

Standard Western Dragon page 46

Tarasque page 48

Worm page 50

Publisher's Foreword

As the publisher of best-selling guides on the care of sheep, chickens, pigs and other common livestock, I was intrigued when I heard about one John Topsell, who raises dragons. I contacted him to determine if he were legitimate.

He is. A distant relative of a seventeenth-century naturalist, John has been raising dragons on his remote property for more than thirty years. Still with him is his prize-winning Rowena, a Standard Western Dragon.

After corresponding for months, he consented to prepare a guide for us. He did just that – and along with it, sent us notes, lists, pictures, and other fragments he has collected over time. My executive editor compiled the materials and our art director oversaw the illustrations.

The result is the book you now hold in your hand – the newest addition to our series of animal-raising guides. We hope you like it.

The Publisher

to the Reader

The definitive treatise on dragons can be found in *The Historie of Serpents* (1608), one of the classic works of natural history penned by my famous ancestor, Edward Topsell. That wonderful piece of writing led to my infatuation with dragons at an early age – a passion that remains with me to this day.

A century after my ancestor wrote, Oliver Goldsmith produced *A History of the Earth and Animated Nature*. In it, the noted author made a shocking statement: "The whole race of dragons," he wrote, "is dwindled down to the Flying Lizard, a little harmless creature that only preys upon insects, and even seems to embellish the forest with its beauty."

Nonsense. Nothing could be farther from the truth. Not to belittle the Flying Lizard, but because many dragons live hundreds of years, those born about the time that book was written remain with us. Dragons can still be found around the globe. Most have mellowed in disposition since ancient days, making it possible for humans to interact with them in a positive way.

Within the past several decades, suppliers of different breeds have sprung up worldwide, and more people each year become interested in these extraordinary creatures. Breeders have even responded to consumer demand by providing miniatures of the different breeds.

This book guides you through all the steps you need to acquire, raise and keep your very own dragon.

John Topsell

part 1
Should You Own a Dragon?

Deciding whether to acquire a dragon is one of the most important choices you'll ever make – because it could be lifelong. Even if you have already made up your mind to make the commitment, read this chapter carefully. Then, once you know the basic dragon families, common reasons people raise dragons, and the conditions for acquiring them, you should ask yourself some hard questions about whether you really want to own one of these unique creatures.

What Is a Dragon?

Since time immemorial, people around the world could describe or draw a dragon. But in different times and places, that dragon would be different from the others – because there are multiple families, forms and breeds of this universal creature with mysterious destructive and creative powers. The various kinds of dragons being bred and raised today derive from those ancient ancestral lines.

Snakes share characteristics with the Basilisk.

Basics

Dragon breeds differ in size, shape, colours, powers and habits, but they all share a common nature:

• Dragons belong to the class Reptilia. "Reptile" means "creeping animal," which does not, though, account for the flight of certain dragons.

• Like their crocodile, turtle, lizard and snake cousins, dragons are cold-blooded, carnivorous, and lay eggs. They also have protective scales and bright, hypnotic eyes.

• But dragons are also unlike their reptilian relatives. Many have wings and breathe fire. Some have a mystical gem behind their eyes, magical blood, and fat that cures blindness. Most grow to immense size and live hundreds of years.

Lizards most resemble the Salamander dragon breed.

Like their dragon relatives, turtles hatch from eggs.

The crocodile is another cousin to the dragon.

Edward Topsell's dragons

In his *The Historie of Serpents* (1608), my famous ancestor, Edward Topsell, describes basic physical variations of dragons. Here are some of his descriptions with the illustrations that correspond to them:

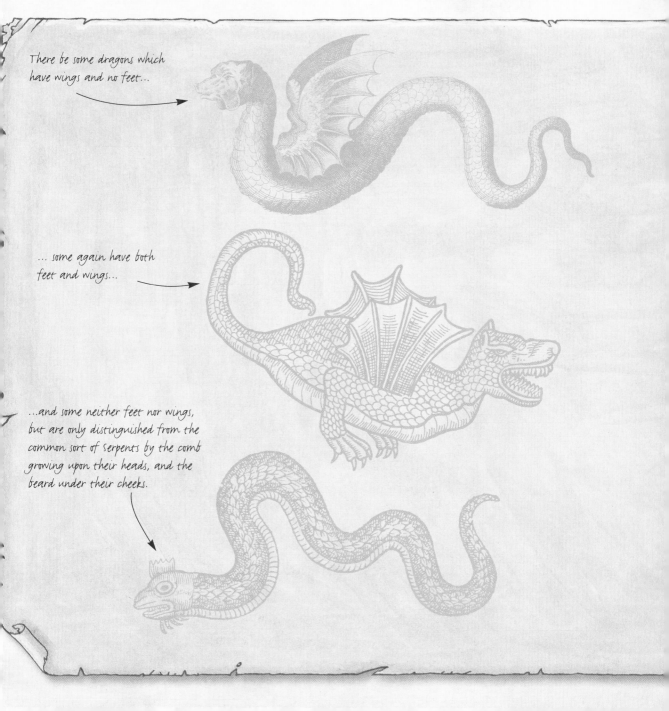

There be some dragons which have wings and no feet...

... some again have both feet and wings...

...and some neither feet nor wings, but are only distinguished from the common sort of serpents by the comb growing upon their heads, and the beard under their cheeks.

Amphiptères and Lindorms

Wyvern

Basilisk

Dragon families

With some variations, my ancestor's categories comprise the major families of dragons:

- Dragons with large wings and no feet are called *Amphiptères*. Those with small wings and no feet are *Lindorms* (Lindworms). Both of these appear in heraldic crests.

- Dragons with wings and two legs are called *Wyverns*. These are also heraldic animals and often appear in medieval and Renaissance paintings. Those with wings and four legs (not pictured by ancestor Topsell) are what I call the Standard Western Dragon (such as my Rowena); it is a common heraldic dragon. Asian and other dragons have four legs and – usually – no wings.

- My ancestor's crested and bearded dragon, without wings or feet (and with very little crest, if any) is similar to the extinct Basilisk, which evolved into the Cockatrice.

- Not included among my ancestor's illustrated dragons are multiheaded dragons, like the Hydra of Lerna. A dragon with no wings and no feet – but with two heads – is an *Amphisbaena*.

Other types of dragons

Outside of the standard dragon families, but related to them, are types of dragons that breeders do not handle and are thus unavailable for raising. One of these is totally inaccessible, shrouded in myth; another can be seen in the night sky.

Tiamat

It's commonly said that dragons are descended from dinosaurs, extinct reptiles with whom some dragons share characteristics of shape and size. A Babylonian creation myth maintains otherwise: In the beginning, the Babylonian she-dragon, Tiamat, was the saltwater of the cosmic abyss. Her mate, Apsu, was the freshwater. The mingling of their waters created a generation of gods whose children killed Apsu. Tiamat vowed vengeance by giving birth to a brood of dragons and other monsters. One of the younger gods, Marduk, confronted her in her cave and shot an arrow into her mouth. Then he split her in half, creating the universe as we know it.

Draco

Look up into the northern sky tonight to see the circumpolar constellation Draco winding its way between the Great Bear and Little Bear. Since ancient times, peoples of the world have claimed the starry dragon as their own:

- To the Babylonians, it was Tiamat.
- To the Greeks, it was the Titanic dragon that Athena hurled into the void during the battle between the Olympians and the Titans; it was also Ladon, which Hercules slew, and the serpent killed by Cadmus, founder of Thebes.
- To the Norse, it was Jörmungandr, the Midgard Serpent. The god Odin threw the young beast into the ocean, where it grew until it encircled the earth, its tail in its mouth.
- To the Persians, it was the man-eating serpent Azhdehā.
- To the Arabs, it was Al Shujā', the Snake.
- And later astronomers interpreted it as the Old Serpent in the Garden of Eden.

Among other dragons in the sky are Hydra the water snake (killed by Hercules) and the sea monster, Cetus, which Perseus slew to rescue Andromeda.

Reasons to Raise a Dragon

Maybe you already know why you want to own a dragon. For those of you who are still wondering whether to have a dragon in your life, consider these excerpts from letters by dragon owners over the years. These are among the most popular reasons for raising dragons.

FOR COMPANIONSHIP

My dragon and I spend a lot of time together on walks on our property. I can't explain it, but there is a mysterious understanding between us.

Yes, if you raise a dragon with care, being attentive to its unique nature and needs, it can become a lifelong friend. My Rowena and I have been together about thirty years, and I can't imagine life without her.

For showing

With more dragon shows cropping up all the time, I encourage other dragon owners to enter their animal into a competition. The training is fun – even though it's rigorous – and I'm convinced that my dragon feels as much pride in winning as I do.

I couldn't agree more. Showing may not be appropriate for all breeds and owners, but it can be most satisfying for both. My prize-winning Rowena is a case in point.

FOR PROFIT

I have rented out my dragon for appearances in shopping centres. The crowds love it, especially the kids.

There are many renting-out possibilities for dragons, but some activities can be risky – for both people and dragons. Three things to keep in mind: the dragon's willingness to participate; insurance to cover the event; and the dragon's safety.

AS A GUARDIAN

I live in a large house out in the country. Even though I employ security guards, I've felt apprehensive about my personal safety, personal treasures, and my property. Now that I have a dragon on the grounds, I have peace of mind.

You don't have to be as affluent as this owner to enjoy the protection of a dragon.

AS AN UNUSUAL "PET"

I've had dogs and cats in the house all my life, but dragons are different. They're so big!

They definitely can be.

FOR TRANSPORTATION

I've ridden horses, ostriches and elephants, but there is nothing so thrilling as riding a flying dragon.

You must, of course, train the dragon properly and have the proper equipment. That goes for any type of dragon-riding – on land or water, as well as in the air.

Some Cautionary Considerations

Now that you know some major advantages to owning a dragon, here are a few possible liabilities you should take into account.

Expense

A rule of thumb: the larger the dragon, the more expensive it will be to raise and care for. Full-sized dragons require exceptional expenditures in terms of special fenced-off areas where they are kept, known as enclosures (some live in deep caves, some beside springs, and others in rivers or large bodies of water) and feed (dragons are enormous eaters). Experts recommend that owners of full-sized dragons be independently wealthy. Others who are less well-off should stick to miniature breeds.

Dragon House, Inc.
Herald Court
Anglesey, Wales

CUSTOMER'S ORDER NO. **720183**

NAME *John Topsell*　　　　　　DATE **May 28**

SOLD BY
- ☑ CASH
- ☐ C.O.D.
- ☐ HOUSE ACCOUNT
- ☐ CREDIT CARD

QUANTITY	DESCRIPTION	AMOUNT
1 truckload	Dragon House Dragon Chow	£800

RECEIVED BY *John Topsell*

KEEP THIS RECEIPT FOR YOUR RECORDS

Last Will and Testament

I, John Topsell, being of sound mind and body, leave my personal and real property (Dragon Village) upon my death to the Dragon Protection League for the superb care of my Standard Western Dragon, Rowena, so long as she shall live (which could be until the twenty-second century — or even longer). . .

John Topsell

Longevity

Since dragons can live for hundreds of years, yours will surely outlive you. This means that unless you sell the animal, you will need to make arrangements for its care following your death.

Attributes

Dragons can be dangerous. Their teeth are like needles, their claws like knives. The fire breathed by certain breeds can burn you or even destroy your home and property. Medical and fire insurance are musts.

Liability

Many dragons of the past were notorious for ravaging the countryside and destroying entire villages. If your dragon remains genetically wired to follow their example, the resulting litigation could bankrupt you. Proper training, a secure enclosure, and liability insurance are essential.

BUILDING ESTIMATE

PARAGON CONSTRUCTION COMPANY

PROPOSAL SUBMITTED TO John Topsell
DATE 29 July

We hereby submit specifications and estimate for:
Dragon cave in hillside:
Entrance 4 m wide x 4 m high
Cave 30 m deep, with chamber 9 m x 9 m x 6 m
Excavation
Bracing

	£20,000
	£3,000

Fence 4 m high x 90 m long:
1 large gate, 1 small
30 steel posts 10 cm dia. 5 m long
30 concrete settings 1 m deep, 1 m dia.

£7,000

Outbuilding 6 m x 6 m:
Fire-resistant walls and roof,
windows on 3 sides, doors on 2
Plumbing, electricity, heating

£28,000

Run water to trough in enclosure

£1,000

We hereby propose to furnish labour and materials in complete accordance with the above specification, for the sum of

£59,000

All material is guaranteed to be as specified. All work is to be completed in a skillful manner according to standard practices.

ROBERTS, TAYLOR, & DAVIS
Solicitors

Mr John Topsell
Dragon Village
Glastonbury
Somerset

Dear Mr Topsell,

This is to inform you that your neighbour, Eugene Clayton, has retained our services in a matter concerning an animal that resides on your property.

At dusk on Saturday last, Mr Clayton returned to his home to find a monstrous creature with a back spiked like the hull of a chestnut standing in his flower bed. In beating a hasty retreat on its many legs, the beast broke through a rose trellis. Then, covered with trellis and pink English roses, it proceeded to crash through a fence separating Mr Clayton's estate from your property.

Wishing to settle out of court, Mr Clayton estimates property damage and mental anguish caused by the creature to total £10,000.

A Checklist of Intent

Along with its joys and rewards, raising a dragon comes with heavy responsibilities. You should decide to acquire a dragon only if you are committed to giving it the care it deserves. So, should you raise a dragon? Here are some questions to help you decide. (If you don't want to mark up this book, write on a photocopied page.)

⁙1⁙

Do I really want to raise and keep a dragon?
(Be honest about this, because if you're not, you – and your dragon – might be in for much grief.)

YES NO

⁙2⁙

Why do I want to raise and keep a dragon?
(Again, be honest.)

A
As a companion, guardian and source of profit.

B
Because I think it would be fun, or just something to do.

C
Other.

⁙3⁙

Am I willing to spend the rest of my life with **this creature?**
(Remember, your dragon will surely outlive you.)

YES NO

If you answered "No" to Question 3, would you assure that your dragon be given a good home?

YES NO

⁙4⁙

If I keep the dragon, will I arrange in my will for its care after my death?

YES NO

⁙5⁙

Can I actually afford to purchase, raise and care for a dragon?
(Expenses will depend on whether you choose a miniature or a full-sized dragon and to some degree on the selection of breed.)

YES NO

⁙6⁙

Can I provide the proper enclosed area for my dragon?
(Again, it will depend on the size and breed you choose. Selection of a full-sized dragon will be determined by the kind of property you have – whether it contains a hill or cliff, a spring, river, or private lake.)

YES NO

⁙7⁙

Am I willing to provide my dragon with whatever kind and amount of food it needs to be healthy and happy?

YES NO

⁙8⁙

Will I be willing to devote the time and energy needed to care for, play with, exercise and train my dragon?

YES NO

IF YOU ANSWERED A TO QUESTION 2 AND "YES" TO ALL THE REST, PROCEED TO THE NEXT PAGE.

part 2
Dragon Breeds

Congratulations. After some honest soul-searching, you have decided to raise and keep a dragon. But first, review the many available breeds to choose from. All these, as the following genealogy chart shows, are descended from the Cosmic Dragon that in ancient stories emerged from Chaos and encircled the world. In this section, I present the variety of modern breeds in guidebook alphabetical order. Among them is the perfect dragon for you.

Genealogy of Breeds

The age-old figure of the Ouroboros is a dragon curled in a circle with its tail in its mouth. It traditionally symbolizes cyclic time or eternity. I use it here, as a border on this old map, to represent the Cosmic Dragon, to which even modern breeds can trace their beginnings.

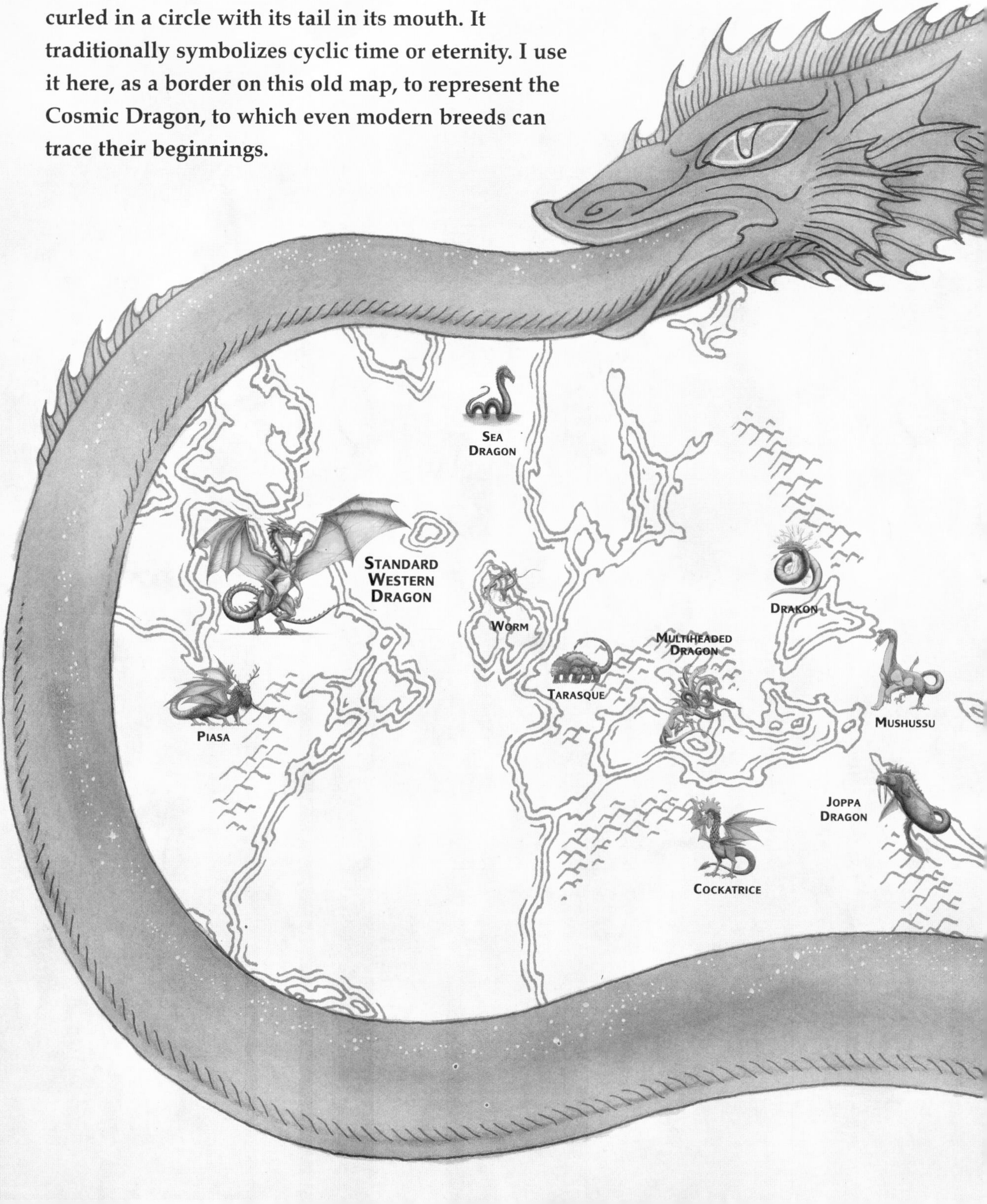

SEA
DRAGON

STANDARD
WESTERN
DRAGON

WORM

DRAKON

MULTIHEADED
DRAGON

TARASQUE

MUSHUSSU

PIASA

JOPPA
DRAGON

COCKATRICE

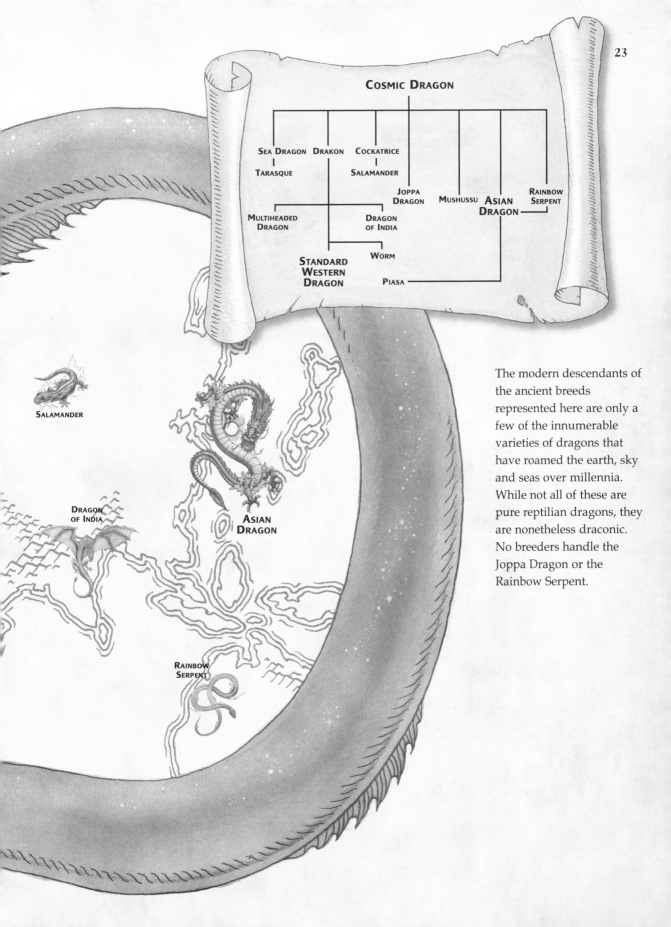

COSMIC DRAGON

SEA DRAGON   DRAKON   COCKATRICE

TARASQUE   SALAMANDER

JOPPA   MUSHUSSU   ASIAN   RAINBOW
DRAGON   DRAGON   SERPENT

MULTIHEADED   DRAGON
DRAGON   OF INDIA

                    WORM

STANDARD
WESTERN   PIASA
DRAGON

SALAMANDER

DRAGON
OF INDIA

ASIAN
DRAGON

RAINBOW
SERPENT

The modern descendants of the ancient breeds represented here are only a few of the innumerable varieties of dragons that have roamed the earth, sky and seas over millennia. While not all of these are pure reptilian dragons, they are nonetheless draconic. No breeders handle the Joppa Dragon or the Rainbow Serpent.

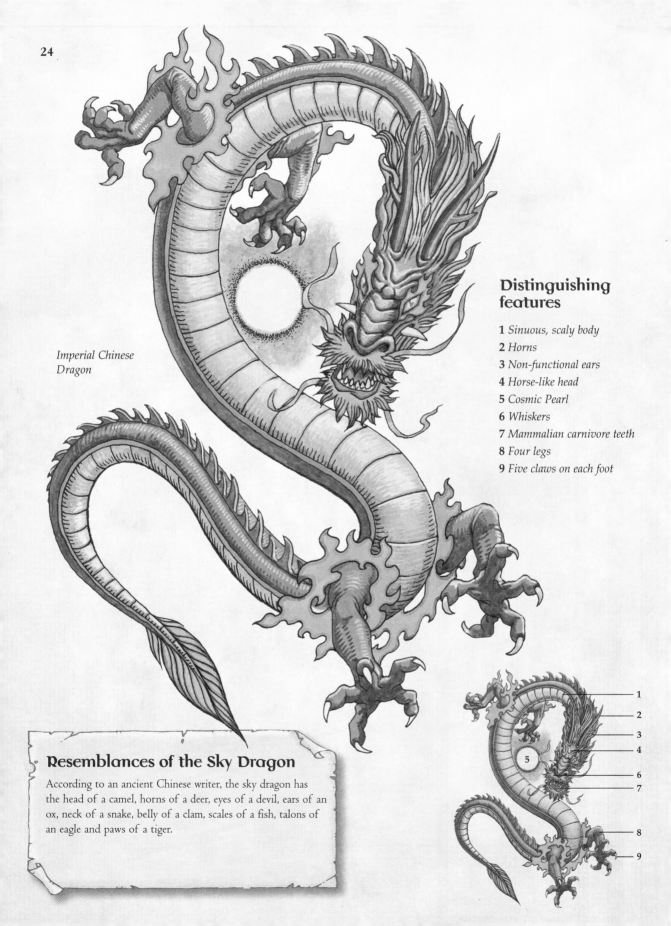

Imperial Chinese Dragon

Distinguishing features

1 *Sinuous, scaly body*
2 *Horns*
3 *Non-functional ears*
4 *Horse-like head*
5 *Cosmic Pearl*
6 *Whiskers*
7 *Mammalian carnivore teeth*
8 *Four legs*
9 *Five claws on each foot*

Resemblances of the Sky Dragon

According to an ancient Chinese writer, the sky dragon has the head of a camel, horns of a deer, eyes of a devil, ears of an ox, neck of a snake, belly of a clam, scales of a fish, talons of an eagle and paws of a tiger.

Asian Dragon
Draco asiaticus

The most exuberant of all dragon breeds, the Asian Dragon is a joyful weather lord, ruling clouds, rain, thunder and lightning. It is the emperor of all scaly creatures, one of the four celestial animals of China, and one of the twelve signs of the Chinese zodiac. Ancient rulers claimed to be incarnations of these divine beings. It's said that somewhere in the cosmos is a tablet containing the number of existing dragons.

Description Whirling, twisting, leaping, the four-legged Asian Dragon is all energy. On its maned, horse-like head are horns that serve as ears. Long whiskers curl from its muzzle. A serrated ridge stretches the length of its scaly body. It can change its form and size at will, expand to fill the sky, shrink to the size of a silkworm – or disappear altogether. Its voice sounds like tinkling bells or the clatter of copper pans. Its favourite food is roasted swallows. The Imperial Chinese Dragon has five claws on each foot, the dragon of commoners four claws, and the Japanese Dragon three.

Attributes This dragon typically chases – or plays with – a bluish white, red, or golden ball of light. Variously interpreted as rolling thunder, the sun, the moon, or the Cosmic Pearl, "the pearl that grants all desires," it is said to contain the animal's power.

Temperament Traditionally, unlike most Western Dragons, the Asian Dragon is a mostly benevolent creature. It fears centipedes, silk of five colours and iron. However, when angered, it has been known to cause typhoons and floods.

Special care Asian Dragon eggs can be purchased, but given the animals' ability to change shape and size, the breed cannot actually be contained or raised in the usual sense. There are, though, special ways to lure an Asian Dragon to your property and become its companion (see pages 73, 102, and 106).

Relatives Different Asian dragons rule the sky, earth and seas – from the sky dragon to dragon kings living in jewelled undersea palaces.

Locator map

The Asian Dragon may have originated in India. From China, it spread to Japan and throughout Southeast Asia (excluding Thailand, however, where the elephant is king).

Egg

The Asian Dragon is within the pearl-like shell for three thousand years. Upon hatching, it instantaneously grows to its full size.

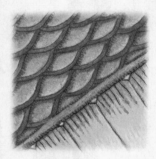

Skin swatch

Scaly skin, typically red or blue

Height/size

Varies from the size of a silkworm to the sky itself

Cockatrice
Draco basileus

In spite of its evolution from the deadly Basilisk, the modern breed of Cockatrice is appealing to a small group of dragon raisers. The bizarre creature looks fearsome but is now harmless and docile. Even its bad breath – unlike its ancestor's – helps make it a cult favorite.

Description Ancient writers described the Basilisk ancestor of this beast as a serpent with a white crown-like spot upon its head. That marking gave the creature its name, a form of which means "king". Not more than one foot (30 cm) in length, it was the King of Small Serpents. As the breed developed, it grew in size and changed in shape, transforming into a Cockatrice, a monstrosity with a crown-shaped crest, cockerel's head, neck and feet, membranous dragon wings and long serpentine tail.

Pedigree The Basilisk was born in Libya from the blood of snake-haired Medusa. Its toxic breath withered all growing things, reducing woodland to desert and even killing birds flying overhead. A Basilisk speared by a knight on horseback was so deadly that its poison, travelling up the spear shaft, killed not only the rider but the horse as well. But this monster, too, could be destroyed. It expired when it saw its own hideous self reflected in a shield or mirror. A weasel luring a Basilisk into its foul den would battle the serpent until both died.

Locator map

Libya and Europe

Egg

Cockatrices are born from spherical eggs laid by seven-year-old cockerels and hatched for nine years by toads or serpents.

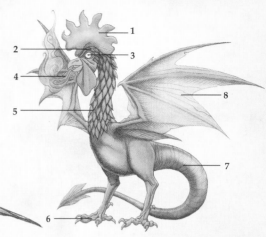

Distinguishing features

1 *Crest*	**5** *Cockerel's neck*
2 *Cockerel's head*	**6** *Cockerel's feet*
3 *Deadly stare*	**7** *Scaly serpentine tail*
4 *Bad breath*	**8** *Membranous wings*

And the crowing of a cockerel would send the reptile into fatal convulsions. It's not surprising that travellers braving the Libyan desert carried cockerels with them.

Attributes When walked down the street on a leash, this colourful monstrosity gets more attention than any pet dog, much to the mischievous delight of the Cockatrice owner.

Special care This breed is not for everybody.

Relatives Icelandic Scoffin; Wyvern.

Height/size

The size of a normal cockerel

Skin swatch

Colourful cockerel feathers

Distinguishing features

1 *Fiery crest*
2 *Shining eyes*
3 *Draconce inside the skull*
4 *Beard*
5 *Two legs*
6 *Scales*
7 *Constrictor body*
8 *Wings*

*Mountain
Dragon of India*

Dragon of India
Draco indicus

The magical gems in the forehead of the Dragon of India attracted greedy hunters in the ancient land of marvels. And many of the breed also expired in battles with a natural enemy. Nonetheless, descendants of the surviving Indian dragons are still in demand among dragon raisers fascinated by the creature's jewels.

Description The Dragon of India is a large serpent. There are two varieties of the breed: marsh dragons and mountain dragons. Those living in marshes are sluggish and their bodies are black. The swift mountain dragons – by far the more popular with dragon raisers – have fiery red crests, beards, gleaming eyes and glittering golden scales. Some of these have two legs and wings. Neither variety is venomous. Their strength is in their tails.

Attributes The mystical gems in the dragon's head are named Draconce. Magical in curative power, they shine in the creature's eyes. While hunters had to kill such dragons for the prize, dragon raisers must be satisfied just to know the jewels are there – unless they outlive their dragon.

Habits Ancestors of the mountain dragon were infamous for lying in wait on rocks or in trees and dropping upon their surprised prey. This dragon's natural enemy was the elephant, which the serpent encoiled with its long constrictor body. When the elephant succumbed from exhaustion, it crushed the dragon as it fell.

Special care The modern breed remains genetically fascinated by elephants. Equipping your dragon's hilly, wooded enclosure with a life-sized stuffed pachyderm will interest your animal and provide it with a means of exercise.

Pedigree point Judges always note the brightness of a dragon's eyes.

Relatives The Dragon of Ethiopia.

Author's Note
On my desk is a Draconce I purchased in Bombay (now Mumbai) years ago; I have not been ill a day since.

Locator map

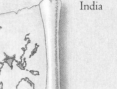

India

Egg

Elephant grey in colour

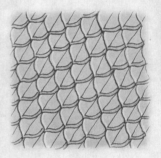

Skin swatch

Scaly in texture and golden in colour

Height/size

Three times the length of a full-grown elephant

Drakon
Draco

To the ancient Greeks, the Drakon was a large serpent. Sharp-eyed and possessing the wisdom of the ages, the ancient ancestors of this breed were renowned as guardians of sacred springs and treasure. Some spoke through the mouths of oracles.

Description The Greek Drakon has no legs or wings. Some have crests, triple rows of teeth and three-forked golden tongues. Their eyes flash with fire. These dragons are poisonous and can crush adversaries with their countless coils of dry, hard scales. They are partial to milk and honey cakes.

Pedigree Associated with the gods, the Drakon has one of the most distinguished ancestral lines of any dragon breed. The Drakon Pytho lived beside a spring on Mount Parnassus until Apollo killed it with his arrows and established his sanctuary as the home of the Delphic Oracle. The Oracle later instructed Cadmus on how to select a site on which to found his city. His quest led him to a Drakon at a spring. After he slew the creature, the

Locator map

Greece (Delphi and Thebes) and formerly found in the ancient country of Colchis on the eastern shore of the Black Sea

Egg

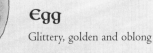

Glittery, golden and oblong

goddess Athena told him to sow its teeth, from which sprung fighting warriors. The survivors helped him build Thebes. Athena then gave some of the dragon's teeth to Jason, who sowed them during his successful quest to obtain the Golden Fleece of Colchis from a sleeping Drakon guardian.

Habits Drakons are a prized breed among dragon raisers because of their divine knowledge and because they loyally – although not always successfully – guard the treasure of others. They do not hoard riches for themselves, as some other breeds do.

Special care To raise a Drakon, you must have a spring on your property.

Pedigree point At shows, a Drakon might speak through a woman you select as an oracle.

Distinguishing features

1 *Crest*
2 *Sharp, watchful eyes*
3 *Triple rows of teeth*
4 *Three-forked golden tongue*
5 *Dry, hard scales*
6 *Coiling body*

1
2
3
4
5
6

Height/size

Described by an ancient writer as "vaster than a ship of 50 oarsmen"

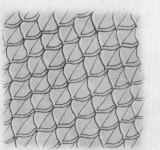

Skin swatch

Dry, hard scales

Cetus Notes

- The skeleton of Cetus was displayed in ancient Rome.
- The marks of Andromeda's chains are still evident in a shore rock at the site of Joppa.
- You can see Perseus, Cetus, Andromeda, and her parents, Queen Cassiopeia and King Cepheus, among a group of constellations.

Distinguishing features

1 *Walrus-like nose*
2 *Blazing eyes*
3 *Crest*
4 *Enormous body*
5 *Coiling, scaly tail*
6 *Flippers*
7 *Tusks*

Joppa Dragon
Draco cetus

No catalogue of dragon breeds would be complete without mention of two of the most famous dragons of all time. Vanquished by Perseus and St George, these monsters were linked by habit and geography. Sightings of their eastern Mediterranean relatives have been reported since, but no suppliers are interested in handling them.

Description Accounts of the older examples of these water monsters vary in detail, but most agree that one she-beast, named Cetus, had a gigantic, whale-like body. Some say she had a scarlet crest, blazing eyes, walrus-like nose, tusks and flippers, and a coiling tail covered with impenetrable scales. Her later relative from the marshes was said to crawl onto land on short legs like a crocodile.

Pedigree As different from each other as the two dragons were, their fates carried them both to the eastern Mediterranean town of Joppa, in ancient Philistia. The hero Perseus was flying homeward on winged sandals when he saw Cetus surging through the water towards the sacrificial Andromeda, chained to a rock. Repeated thrusts of his sword into the beast's thick hide saved the damsel.

Only miles away from that legendary site is the tomb of St George, later patron saint of England. Crusaders who fought at Joppa took back to Europe the tale of the young George coming upon a girl being sacrificed to a marsh dragon. After George subdued the demon with his spear, the girl led it into town, where it met its death at the hands of the villagers.

Habits It's hardly necessary to point out obvious similarities between the actions of the two dragons – and the two heroes.

Temperament Also obvious.

Special care The treatment of both Cetus and the marsh dragon is part of a long human tradition that modern dragon raisers are advised not to share with their other breeds of dragons.

Locator map

Ancient city of Joppa, in Palestine

Egg

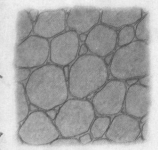

Reddish in colour; shell pattern imitates Cetus's swimming motion

Skin swatch

Hard, heavy scales

Height/size

As large as a blue whale: 66–98 feet (20–30 m)

Distinguishing features

1 *Serpent heads, varying in number*
2 *Long scaly necks*
3 *Poisonous fangs*
4 *Forked tongue*

Hydra

Multiheaded Dragon

Draco hydrus

The most physically repulsive of all dragons, those with multiple heads are little in demand by dragon raisers. The Greek supplier of the breed reports that the few full-sized ones he has sold appear in carnival sideshows and sword-and-sandal adventure films. Miniatures sell better because they are not as intimidating.

Description The generic name identifies this breed's prominent characteristic. The serpent heads growing from long sinuous necks vary in number, but seven or nine are the most common. The heads emit a foul smoke, accompanied by hissing and a flickering of forked tongues.

Pedigree Such dragons are descended from an irregular ancestral line beginning with the monstrous offspring of the multiheaded Typhon and the snake-woman Echidna. They spawned the lion/goat/serpent-headed Chimera, the three-headed dog Cerberus, and the many-headed, reptilian Hydra of Lerna, whom Hercules slew. The renowned Greek hero also vanquished others of the breed: hundred-headed Ladon and the octopus-like Scylla. Yet another of the breed was the Great Red Dragon of the Apocalypse, with its seven crowned heads and ten horns; Michael and his angels cast it and its followers out of heaven.

Temperament A psychiatrist friend of mine explained to me why even the current breed of Multiheaded Dragons tends to be vicious: they nurse a deep, lifelong anger at being one of a loathsome breed. They are difficult to train.

Special care When they are hired out, full-sized members of this breed must be heavily guarded. Miniatures' multiple heads should be muzzled (a difficult task). Miniatures must be protected from other domestic pets, because for every head that is bitten off, two will grow.

Locator map

Greece (Hydra), Italy (Scylla), and Northwest Africa (Ladon)

Egg

Soft, brown shell with bumpy surface

Skin swatch

Scaly yet flexible

Height/size

Varies from twice the size of a Greek hero to a hundred times larger

Mushussu
Draco babylonicus

Represented on the Ishtar Gate of Babylon, the Mushussu (also known as Sirrush) was a guardian and companion of the gods. It is one of the oldest of dragon breeds and is the most loyal of all. Resembling a small horse more than a conventional dragon, this graceful, long-legged creature is a favourite among dragon raisers.

Description The Mushussu is a mixture of several animals. It has a snake's forked tongue, and its long neck and tail are those of a serpent. Reptilian scales cover its elongated body. Horns curl from its head, and a trifold flap hangs from its neck. Its forelegs and paws are those of a lion, its hind legs and taloned feet those of an eagle.

Pedigree The ancestor of the modern Mushussu was the consort of many Babylonian gods and was the sacred animal of the god Marduk, who slew the great she-dragon Tiamat and created heaven and earth from her body. When Nebuchadnezzar II built his palace in honour of Marduk, he depicted the Mushussu – along with common lions and bulls – on the great Ishtar Gate and along the Sacred Way. The famous Hanging Gardens of Babylon was one of the Seven Wonders of the ancient world. After the city fell and was covered by desert sands, the Mushussu was forgotten for two thousand years – until a German archeological team excavated the city. On its reconstructed walls, the figure of the Mushussu proudly strode again. Since that time, the breed has evolved from its rare survivors.

Locator map
Iraq

Egg
Scaly and green

Attributes The Mushussu is a loyal companion and guardian and is good with children. Due to its divine lineage and regal bearing, it is a frequent winner at dragon shows.

Special care This distinguished dragon deserves a palatial enclosure and considerate care.

Relatives Some cryptozoologists identify it with the *mokele-mbembe*, a saurian survivor.

Distinguishing features

1 *Curled horns*	**7** *Serpent neck*
2 *Forked tongue*	**8** *Ridge down neck*
3 *Scaly body*	**9** *Serpentine tail*
4 *Lion forelegs*	**10** *Eagle hind legs*
5 *Lion paws*	**11** *Eagle talons*
6 *Trifold flap*	

Skin swatch

Small green and golden scales

Height/size

The height of a young bull

Piasa
Draco piasarus

Of all the dragon breeds, the Piasa (PIE-ah-saw) is the most bizarre in appearance. It's as though nature selected parts of a variety of beasts and combined them all in this creature. The full-sized Piasa is fearsome; its miniature variety is a novelty. In any case, the breed is a cult favourite among those who raise dragons.

Description French priest Jacques Marquette was the first to describe the Piasa. While exploring North America's Mississippi River in 1673, he and his companion, Louis Joliet, saw images of two grotesque figures on a cliff face above a stretch of turbulent water. Painted in red, black and green, each beast was: "as large as a calf, with horns like a deer, red eyes, a beard like a tiger and a frightful expression of countenance. The face is something like that of a man, the body covered with scales; and the tail so long that it passes entirely round the body, over the head and between the legs, ending like that of a fish."

Locator map
United States (Illinois)

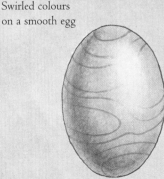

Egg
Swirled colours
on a smooth egg

Skin swatch
Green and gold scales

Pedigree A local Algonquin Indian tribe called the monster Piasa, meaning "the bird which devours men". In legend, it carried off members of the tribe until warriors ambushed it and killed it with poison arrows. The original rock art of the Piasa is gone from the site that is near the town of Alton, Illinois, but the composite beast now glares from a restored painting on a bluff overlooking the river.

Temperament The violent strain of the Piasa that terrorized the Illini Algonquins has been weakened over time by careful breeding. When it first appears at dragon shows, a full-grown Piasa frightens the spectators, but a miniature is an immediate crowd-pleaser.

Special care The ideal enclosure for a full-grown Piasa contains cliffs above a turbulent river. Accommodations for miniatures of this breed can be made in a Dragon Room.

Relatives The North American Horned Serpent; Chinese and Japanese dragons.

Distinguishing features

1 *Leathery wings*	4 *Antlers*	7 *Taloned bird's feet*
2 *Red eyes*	5 *Fangs*	8 *Scaly body*
3 *Man-like face*	6 *Beard*	9 *Long, scorpion-like tail*

Height/size

Father Marquette said the Piasa in the painting was the size of a calf. Others have said the body of the creature is 15 feet (4.5 m) long and its tail is at least 50 feet (15 m) in length. The full-grown Piasa is closer in size to the latter estimate.

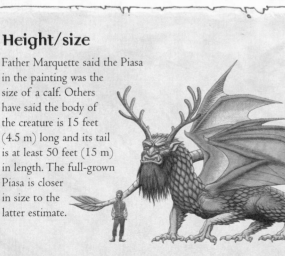

Author's Note
When I visited Alton years ago, a local man took me out in his rowing boat to see the modern painted version of the monster Father Marquette described.

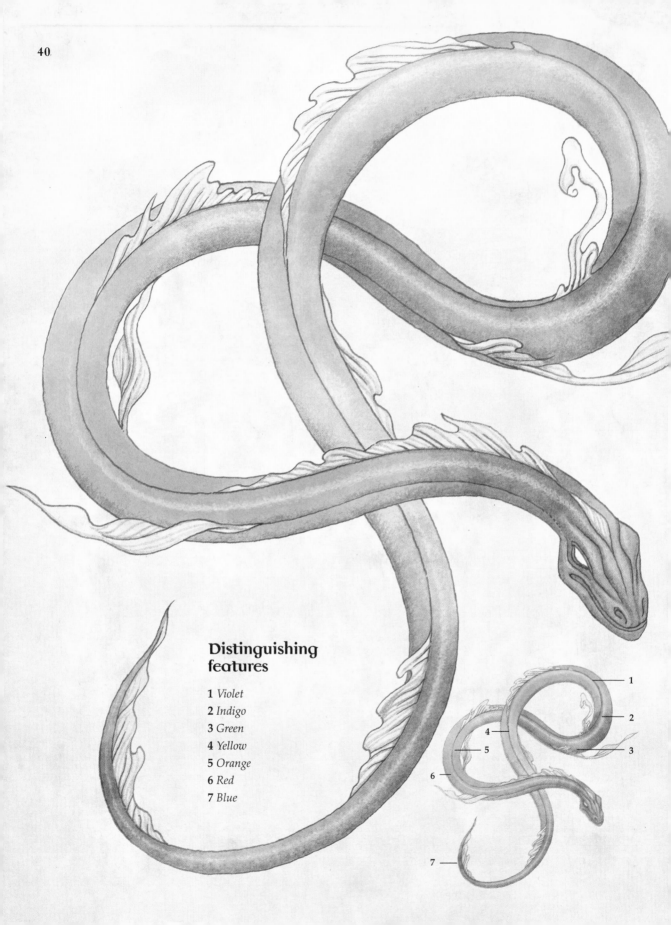

Distinguishing features

1 *Violet*
2 *Indigo*
3 *Green*
4 *Yellow*
5 *Orange*
6 *Red*
7 *Blue*

Rainbow Serpent
Draco arcus

Revered – and sometimes feared – by peoples around the world, the Rainbow Serpent is one of the most majestic of dragon breeds. We have all seen its shining, multicoloured body arcing through mist or dark skies. Unfortunately, because this dragon cannot be contained, no breeder handles it. But it's possible that a Rainbow Serpent may visit your property – as one occasionally appears on mine.

Description Rainbow Serpents are vast and beautiful python-like creatures with striped markings of all colours. An Australian variation of the breed has a head resembling that of a kangaroo. These dragons have also lived in Malaysia, the South Pacific, the Americas, the Congo and West Africa.

Pedigree An aboriginal rock painting dating from about six thousand years ago depicts one of the breed that formed Australia's mountains, valleys, lakes and rivers as it moved over the land. Another Rainbow Serpent, Aido Hwedo, shaped West Africa. It was the first creature made by the god Mawu, and it still lies curled at the bottom of the sea, supporting the world.

Habits Rainbow Serpents typically sleep in deep lakes and pools during dry seasons and rise into the sky to drink the spring rains. They then curve back to earth. They are generally benevolent, but become so angry when they are awakened during droughts that they raise devastating floods. In the aboriginal prehistoric Dreamtime, a fisherman disturbed a Rainbow Serpent slumbering in a lake, causing the Great Flood that washed away villages and covered the earth.

Special care If you have a waterfall or deep pools on your property, or if you live on the shores of a lake, you may be so fortunate as to see a Rainbow Serpent up close from time to time. While it's impossible to train such a dragon, you should know that the creature is fond of shells, pearls and other objects that – like itself – shine with iridescent light. Gifts of these placed beside the dragon's resting places may entice it to rise.

Relatives Rain Dragons of China.

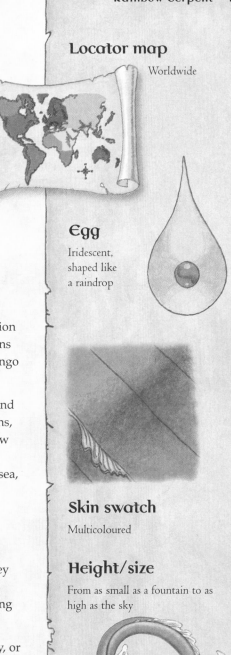

Locator map

Worldwide

Egg

Iridescent, shaped like a raindrop

Skin swatch

Multicoloured

Height/size

From as small as a fountain to as high as the sky

Salamander
Draco salamandra

Smallest of all dragons, the Salamander is renowned for its ability to live in fire. It is also one of the most deadly of the reptilian race. Its lethal nature, though, makes it the breed of choice among a small number of dragon raisers who are particularly attracted to danger – and to its valuable Salamander Wool.

Description The Salamander is a scaly, four-legged dragon covered with spots. Only inches in length, its unremarkable lizard-like appearance disguises its imperviousness to fire and its noxious nature. Given the already small size of the creature, breeders have not produced a miniature variety.

Pedigree The Salamander is so cold that when it crawls into flames (presumably to warm itself), it puts out the fire. Also, a frothy substance exuding from its mouth poisons anything it touches.

Attributes Salamanders have been seen basking in molten lava at the base of volcanoes. In the kingdom of Prester John, Emperor of all the Indias, the creatures lived in such a fiery mountain, producing Salamander Wool, an asbestos-like substance woven into fire-resistant cloth. On the other hand, they can destroy entire communities. By climbing apple trees, they infect the fruit that people eat, and by falling into wells, they poison water supplies.

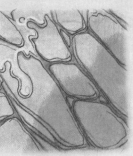

Locator map

The Kingdom of Prester John, variously located from Ethiopia to China

Egg

White, with the texture of Salamander Wool; sits in a nest of flame

Skin swatch

Scaly with spots. Beware of Salamander poison.

Special care Anyone who raises a Salamander must provide the animal with a source of heat, preferably a massive fire in which it can immerse itself without extinguishing the entire blaze. If the creature produces Salamander Wool, the dragon raiser can gather the substance and sell it. But Salamander owners must take care that they are not infected by the dragon's poison.

Pedigree points A Salamander adept at spinning Salamander Wool will impress judges, but here's a caution: The participating dragon raiser has to prevent anyone and virtually anything from coming in contact with the toxic creature.

Relatives The Pyralis, an insect that lives in fire.

Distinguishing features

1 *Scaly body*
2 *Spots*
3 *Four legs*
4 *Poisonous froth*

Height/size

5–6 inches (13–15 cm)

Author's Note

The only salamander I ever raised once escaped from my property. I nervously looked for the poisonous beast for days – until the local blacksmith complained to me that the fire in his forge kept burning out. I found my salamander among the coals, picked it up with the smith's tongs, and carried it home in a box lined with salamander wool.

Sea Dragon
Draco mare

Also known as the Sea Serpent, the Sea Dragon breed is popular among dragon raisers living on the shores of private lakes. Such lakes are natural enclosures, unlike coastal areas from whose waters this dragon would roam free throughout the oceans of the world – and perhaps they already do.

Description The Sea Dragon swims with its long neck held high, like a pillar. It has a horse-like head, fiery eyes and a long mane resembling seaweed. Its scaly vertical coils roll along behind, undulating on the water.

Pedigree A well-known early Sea Dragon appears on Olaus Magnus' 1539 map of Scandinavia. Two hundred feet (60 m) long, the dragon on the map coils around a ship, a sailor in its jaws. Since then, Sea Dragons have been sighted by hundreds of sailors and others. These reported sightings have occurred off the coast of Norway, in the lochs of Scotland, across the North Atlantic, and in oceans and lakes around the globe.

Temperament Most modern members of the breed are shy animals that avoid human contact. This reticence would make them unsuitable for dragon shows. But the dragon raiser who earns a Sea Dragon's trust should be able to ride the animal.

Special care Dragon raisers who choose to own a full-sized Sea Dragon must inform neighbours that a harmless reptile lives in your private lake. They need to be advised that if they have the good fortune to see it through mist or by moonlight, they need not be frightened and must not harm it in any way. A miniature of the breed can be kept in a large aquarium stocked with fish and seaweed.

Relatives The so-called "monster" of Loch Ness.

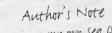

Author's Note
Years before acquiring my own Sea Dragon, I shivered with other seekers at a tour-boat rail, peering into the mist of Loch Ness to get a glimpse of the wondrous creature said to live in the lake's murky depths. It did not appear that day.

Distinguishing features

1 *Horse-like head*
2 *Fiery eyes*
3 *Mane*
4 *Scaly body*
5 *Vertical coils*

Locator map

Western coast
of Norway, Scotland,
North Atlantic

Egg

Undulating
vertical coils
encircle the
eggshell

Skin swatch

Scaly skin

Height/size

40–200 feet
(12–60 m)

Standard Western Dragon
Draco generis

For want of a better term, the Standard Western Dragon is my name for the best-known and most popular dragon breed in Europe and now in much of North America as well.
It is the variety that most Westerners envision when they see or hear the word "dragon".

Description The largest of all serpents, the Standard Western Dragon is a scaly reptile with broad spiny wings, four legs and a long serpentine tail. Its teeth and claws are cutting sharp. It usually has horns, and sometimes its tongue and tail are barbed. Keen of sight and acute of hearing, it has watchful eyes and pointed ears. It breathes smoke and fire, and its roar shakes the ground. This breed can live hundreds of years.

Habits The Standard Western Dragon hoards and guards treasure in deep caves. In medieval

Egg
Green, red, or brown, scaly, hot to the touch, seeping smoke

Locator map
Europe, United States and southern Canada

Skin swatch
Scaly; any of various colours

Europe, ancestors of the present breed were equally renowned for ravaging the countryside, burning villages, and assaulting maidens. The breed's destructive activities inevitably led to battles with knights – and usually to the deaths of the dragons.

Temperament Because the most violent of the winged four-legged dragons came to a bad end, their strain of the breed eventually died out. Individuals of the current, gentler breed make faithful companions and are good with children.

Special care Despite their general docility, modern Standard Western Dragons retain the strength, sharp claws, and fire-breathing capability of their ancestors. Also, genetic traces of ferocity occasionally – but rarely – surface. In any case, the dragon raiser must always be attentive to the moods of his or her dragon.

Relatives The closest relative of the Standard Western Dragon is the winged, two-legged Wyvern.

Distinguishing features

1 *Scaly reptilian body, variable in colour*
2 *Long serpentine tail, sometimes barbed*
3 *Blade-sharp claws, four on each foot*
4 *Bristled or plated back-ridge*
5 *Saddle area*
6 *Ribbed, membranous wings*
7 *Curved claws on wingtips*
8 *Horns*
9 *Bright hypnotic eyes, transparent lids*
10 *Source of combustible phosphorus*
11 *Flared, smoke-emitting nostrils*
12 *Blade-sharp teeth*
13 *Source of earthshaking roar*

Height/size

A full-sized dragon would fill a small house.

Dragon Fire

My longtime friend and internationally known natural historian, Dr Nels Erikson, once sent me an explanation of the phenomenon:

> *Dragons produce fire through a complex chemistry. The highly flammable element of phosphorus resides in glands in a dragon's lower jaw. When a dragon contracts its fire glands, phosphorus is squeezed into the animal's mouth, where it mixes with saliva and — voila! — explodes into flame.*

Dr Erikson goes on to note that the bombardier beetle shoots a jet of gas the temperature of boiling water — not as spectacular as dragon fire-breathing, but definitely disconcerting to predators.

Note: *It is difficult to train a dragon when not to breathe fire, but the dragon raiser must do the best he or she can, especially if the animal will appear in public — namely in dragon shows.*

Tarasque
Draco tarascus

Each year in Tarascon, France, villagers celebrate their ancestors' vanquishing of the monstrous Tarasque by parading a cloth effigy of the beast through the streets of the town.

Description The size of a large ox, the amphibious Tarasque is a lion-headed dragon with a spiked, leathery shell on a scaly body. It has six legs, the paws of a bear and a barbed serpentine tail.

Pedigree The lineage of the Tarasque has been traced back to the sea-beast Leviathan and the bonnacon, an ox-like creature who killed hunters with its flaming excrement. The most famous of the Tarasque breed roamed the Rhône Valley in southern France during medieval times. It sank ships in the river and attacked travellers in the surrounding forests. When it went so far as to carry off villagers, people of the victimized town enlisted the

Locator map

France

Egg

Spiked, leathery, brown shell.
Note: *The spikes develop after the egg is laid.*

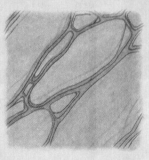

Skin swatch

Leathery shell on scaly body

Distinguishing features

1 *Spikes*
2 *Barbed serpentine tail*
3 *Six legs*
4 *Leathery shell*
5 *Lion head*
6 *Scaly body*
7 *Bear's paws*

aid of St Martha, who had converted them from paganism. Martha entered the wood and found the Tarasque devouring another victim. She sprinkled the beast with holy water, tied her belt around its neck and led it back to town. The villagers killed it and were so elated that they changed the name of their village from Nerluc to Tarascon, after the menace they had overcome.

Temperament Full-grown Tarasques who have learned of their ancestor's fate and its subsequent ridicule tend to be angry creatures. On the other hand, miniatures are good with children and show well.

Special care Enclosures of full-sized Tarasques must contain a river. Only a receptacle of water is required for a miniature. Caution: Avoid the sharp spikes of the dragon, regardless of its size.

Relatives The Tarasca of Spain, whose likeness also highlights a festival procession.

Height/size

The size of a large ox

Author's Note
I attended a Tarascon festival a few years ago and saw the cloth likeness of the beast gaily led through the town with three men supplying the six legs.

Relative

The German *Wurm*, Fafnir, who guarded the Ring of the Nibelungs. After Siegfried killed the beast and ate its heart, he could understand the language of birds.

Distinguishing features

1 *Four legs*
2 *Exceptionally long body*
3 *Steel-hard scales*
4 *Some have wings*
5 *Claws*
6 *No horns*
7 *Smoke and fire*
8 *Needle-sharp fangs*

Worm
Draco britannicus

Worm Hill, Wormstone, Wormingford and Wormsley are a British hill and villages named after a dragon breed that once infested England. While early Worms were notorious for terrorizing the countryside and hoarding treasure, their descendants tend to be lethargic, content to coil around hills and sleep in the sun.

Description The Worm is the British form of the Standard Western Dragon. While some Worms are greater in length than the more generic variety, they, too, are fire-breathing, four-legged reptiles with steel-hard scales. Many have wings and razor-sharp teeth and claws.

Pedigree The most famous of all British Worms was the treasure-hoarding dragon that the ageing Beowulf killed – and was killed by. Later members of the breed were the Lambton Worm and the Dragon of Wantley. Both of these were slain by knights who had attached spikes to their armour. It was the Lambton Worm after whom Worm Hill, near Durham, was named. King Arthur adopted the breed as his insignia and Worms became the heraldic device of British kings.

Special care Dragon raisers who select a full-sized Worm must have a large hill on their property for their dragon to stretch out upon and a deep cave into which it can retreat. This could be a considerable expense for a Worm owner, something that should be taken into account when selecting this breed. For the Worm's pleasure, the dragon raiser should supply the cave with either genuine or imitation treasure.

Pedigree points Due to their long history in Britain, Worms are particularly popular at English shows and are a favourite among English dragon raisers – especially since the modern members of the Worm breed are better behaved than their ancestors were.

Locator map
England

Egg
Green conical egg with spiralling ridges

Skin swatch
Steel-hard scales

Height/size
Long enough to wrap around Worm Hill three times

part 3
Raising the perfect Dragon

Now that you have a general knowledge of dragons and the breeds available from suppliers, you are ready to select the breed you want to raise. The next step is finding and contacting a supplier who handles that breed – and ordering the dragon that will change your life. You'll name it, register it and prepare its enclosure. With its arrival at your home, the adventure of actually raising your very own dragon begins.

Choosing Your Dragon

Which dragon is best for you? Which breed meets your personal preference in physical characteristics, pedigree and temperament or habits? Which breed and size can you house and afford to raise? Whatever your choices, remember that when you acquire a dragon, you also accept responsibility for raising and caring for the creature.

Raising a miniature

If you are not financially independent and you live in an average house or apartment, you should acquire a miniature, not a full-sized, dragon. Keep in mind, though, that your dragon will need a room of its own (see "Indoor Habitats", pages 66–69) and that housing and raising expenses will exceed those of other domestic animals.

Raising a full-sized dragon

Do you have the considerable financial resources and property needed to acquire (they're expensive) and raise (very expensive) a full-sized dragon? Can you accommodate an earth or water dragon – or provide the necessary aviary-like enclosure for a sky dragon? Will planning regulations permit the housing needed for your animal?

The table on this page can help you choose which breed to acquire. If no single kind of dragon matches all the categories, the breed receiving the most tick marks is probably the one for you.

Which Breed Is for You?

First study the Dragon Breeds section on pages 24–51. Then tick the appropriate boxes in terms of your breed preferences and your resources to house and raise a member of that breed.

Breeds	Physical Characteristics	Pedigree	Temperament and Habits	Property	Financial Resources
Asian Dragon					
Cockatrice					
Dragon of India					
Drakon					
Multiheaded					
Mushussu					
Piasa					
Salamander					
Sea Dragon					
Western Dragon					
Tarasque					
Worm					

Your choice of breed: _____

Miniature ☐   Full size ☐

Note: Dragons included in the Breeds section but not handled by breeders are absent from this list. They are the Joppa Dragon and the Rainbow Serpent.

Dragon Selection Guidelines

Now that you have selected the breed you want to raise, decide whether you want to acquire a dragon egg, or a juvenile or adult (age two or older). Then consult the Resources section (pages 122–123) for a breeder/supplier specializing in the dragon of your choice. Upon your purchase of a dragon, the breeder is obligated to provide you with registration papers citing its breed, father and mother, and the date and place of its laying or hatching. The breeder must also guarantee to replace any egg that does not hatch.

Egg guide

If you want to enjoy the total experience of raising your dragon, begin with an egg – which you will then incubate and hatch. Prior to delivery of an egg, the breeder will send you a photograph of a sample egg for your approval. Confirm that the egg matches the breed of dragon you want. The eggs pictured on these pages are representative examples of the different egg colours and shapes of various breeds. For eggs of other kinds of dragons, refer to entries in the Breeds section (pages 24–51).

Standard Western Dragon

The scaly eggs of these fire-breathing, scaly creatures are streaked with green, red or brown – the colours of the dragons themselves. The eggs are hot, and smoke seeps through the shells.

Drakon

Like the Golden Fleece that one of this wise and ancient breed guarded, golden Drakon eggs glitter and shine.

Worm

Ridges spiralling around green conical eggs reflect the Worm habit of coiling around hills to bask in the sun.

Multiheaded Dragon

Moving heads within the eggs of this unpleasant breed push up against the soft brown shells, creating a bumpy surface.

Tarasque

After a Tarasque's egg is laid, spikes emerge from the leathery brown shell, resembling the back of the creature.

Asian Dragon

The eggs of Asian Dragons are as round and luminous as the Cosmic Pearls the energetic, serpentine creatures joyfully pursue. And, like these dragons that change their size at will, the eggs can contract or expand. It can take as long as three thousand years for an Asian Dragon egg to hatch.

Selecting a dragon on site

If you choose to purchase a juvenile or adult dragon – and if you have the financial resources for travel – by all means visit the breeder in person and select your dragon on site. If you do that, here are some basic things to look for to ensure that your animal is healthy. Pictured here is a Standard Western Dragon, which you can use as a general model for your breed of choice.

Plated ridge
If your desired dragon is missing ridge plates, check that the bases have healed properly.

Bright eyes
Dragons are renowned for their sharpness of sight and hypnotic gaze. Dull eyes may indicate a dull animal.

Coughing or sneezing
Listen carefully for sounds of wheezing in the lungs. Breathing should be light and regular when the dragon is in a relaxed state.

Moist nostrils
This is especially important for fire-breathing dragons. Constricted nasal passages cause breathing problems.

Shiny scales
The scales of some dragon breeds shine more than others, but overall, scale glossiness exemplifies good health.

Glossy claws
An important health indicator. Check for small cracks and broken tips. Trimming claws is one of the duties of a dragon raiser.

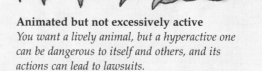

Animated but not excessively active
You want a lively animal, but a hyperactive one can be dangerous to itself and others, and its actions can lead to lawsuits.

Proportion
Regardless of the breed you choose to raise, each part of the animal should be in proper proportion to the other parts.

Vivid colouring
While breeds and parts of individuals differ in tint or hue, the more healthy the animal, the more vivid its colouring.

Intact wings
Examine the wings of a flying creature for signs of former injury that could affect its flight.

Strength
This is the most important attribute of any dragon, regardless of breed or age. After you have examined the animal in detail, ask the breeder to induce it to move so that you can assess its physical ability.

No parasites
Carefully check all bodily openings: mouth, nostrils, ears and vent. Examine droppings for worms.

Full, rounded legs and tail
In breeds with legs and long tails, fullness of legs and tail is an indicator of the animal's health and strength.

Naming Your Dragon

You might already have a name in mind for the dragon you just purchased. If not, you could begin thinking about possible names now, or you could wait until your dragon arrives so that you can observe its individual habits and personality. In any case, you will need a name to register your animal with the Worldwide Dragon Club (see the WDC registration form, with instructions for completion, on pages 62–63).

WDC guidelines

This global registry requires a dragon name of no more than 35 characters. The full name consists of the supplier's company name and the "call name" you choose for your dragon. The combined names comprise a thumbnail history of your animal. If for any reason the WDC finds your submitted name unacceptable, the registry reserves the right to supply one of its own.

Author's Note
I acquired my Rowena as an older juvenile from Dragon House in Wales. Her full WDC registration name is "Dragon House Rowena".

Tips for naming your dragon

Choice of a call name for your dragon is a personal matter, but remember, most dragons are long-lived, and both of you could live with the name for the rest of your lives. Here are a few naming guidelines to consider:

- If your dragon is too young for its gender to be determined, keep the name neuter.
- The "call name" should be short enough for your dragon to recognize it immediately. Some experts say the ideal animal name ends with a vowel.
- While it's popular to make up a fantasy name ending in "th", that's only one kind of name to choose from. Other categories of possible given names are qualities, characteristics, place of origin, flowers, animals, mythological and historical figures, actors, athletes or fictional characters. Please, though, be sensitive to your dragon's feelings and do not call it Apollo, Perseus, Beowulf, Siegfried or George.

Categories of Names

Qualities and characteristics
Smoky, Spike, Flash, Fang, Beauty

Place of origin
Mumbai, Beijing, Alton, Anglesey

Given names and nicknames
Missy, Phoebe, Wanda, Malcolm, Nick

Flowers and animals
Rose, Iris, Daisy, Robin, Tiger

Mythological and historical
Zeus, Thor, Achilles, Ulysses, Helen

Contemporary
Bogie, Beckham, Mickey, Minnie

- While a human name is acceptable for your dragon, I would advise against using your own name. Both you and your dragon would become confused if a third party were to address either of you.
- I do not advise calling your dragon by the name of a living relative. That individual might be offended (even though he or she should be honoured).
- Avoid names such as "Bo", "Kit" or "Neil", which sound similar to commands (e.g., "No", "Sit" and "Heel"). These may confuse your dragon during training.

Which name did you choose?

_____

Full registry name:

_____

Worldwide Dragon Club

Founded in 1900, the WORLDWIDE DRAGON CLUB is dedicated to the breeding and welfare of purebred dragons. It is the oldest and largest all-breed dragon registry on the planet, and keeps records for the convenience of dragon owners everywhere. Here's what the helpful organization says about itself:

"Fittingly enough, we are located near the site at which legend says Tiamat, the Mother of all Dragons, changed from a shapeless saltwater creature of the primal sea into dragon form and was slain by the god Marduk. From her body (the legend continues), Marduk created the earth and sky.

"We are pleased that you are interested in registering your dragon with us, and invite you to contact us should you have any questions or if we can, in any way, be of further assistance to you and your dragon."

❖ GUIDELINES ❖
For completing the WDC registry form

You must take great care in filling out the WDC registry form for your purebred dragon because we reserve the right to reject the application on the grounds of inaccuracy or misrepresentation.

1. Name Very important. Add to your supplier's company name any call name you choose. Both together comprise your dragon's registry name.

2. Breed This must be correct. You should verify your supplier's information through your own research.

3. Sex Aside from variations in dragon colour and size, a dragon's sex can be determined only by a trained observer's examination of the dragon's cloaca (the cavity into which both the intestinal and genitourinary tracts empty).

4. Date of birth If you hatched the egg yourself, simply consult your own records. If you acquired an older dragon, you must accept the information provided by your supplier, but remember: the older the dragon the more approximate the birth date, because dragons can live for hundreds of years.

5. Father and mother Obtain this information from your supplier.

6. Identifying photographs and paw/claw print The form is self-explanatory.

7. Signature Your signature confirms that, to the very best of your knowledge, everything you have entered on the application form is accurate and that your dragon is a purebred animal.

WDC

REGISTRATION APPLICATION

Print in dragon-green ink only. Complete the form and return it to WDC.

Name of dragon for registration: _____

Breed: _____

Sex: _____

Date of birth: _____

Sire: _____Dam: _____

Breeder's/supplier's name: _____

Address: _____

Town and county: _____

Country: _____

Attach two photographs of your dragon here:
(both front and side views required)

Place the paw/claw print of the dragon adjacent to the photographs.
If you acquired a full-grown dragon and its print will not fit on this
page, attach additional sheets.

Owner's name (print): _____

Address: _____

Town and county: _____ Country: _____

I hereby certify that I am the rightful owner of the purebred dragon pictured above,
and that all information is accurate to the best of my knowledge:

Owner's signature: _____ Date: _____

Send this application to WDC at the address below, and, subject to the
approval of our judges, we will register your dragon and send you
a Certificate of Merit.

Worldwide Dragon Club
P.O. Box 111
Mesopotamia BC 30003

Housing Basics

Before your dragon arrives, you will need to prepare its new habitat. The dragon's health and happiness depend upon housing that satisfies its physical and emotional needs. Inexperienced owners of full-sized dragons are often surprised at the size of the enclosure required and the total housing cost, which can far exceed the initial cost of the dragon. Following are environmental necessities for raising and caring for your dragon, whether it is full-sized or a miniature.

Space

Hatchlings and juveniles grow fast, and most dragons of any age or size are naturally curious and love to roam. The more room your dragon has to move around, the better. Several dragon raisers with whom I've corresponded have told me that their dragons were irritable, even mean, before their enclosures were expanded. The more spacious the dragons' surroundings, the more companionable the animals became.

Heat

In preparing housing for your dragon, you must understand the reptilian nature of this creature. Like their cold-blooded reptilian cousins, dragons are ectothermic, meaning that they produce so little of their own body heat that they rely on their environment to supply it.

Note: *Fire-breathing does not affect a dragon's body heat, just as the temperature of a defensive bombardier beetle does not change when it emits a smoking stream of hot, caustic liquid.*

Your dragon will appreciate a good basking spot.

Ample heat (at least 85°F, 29°C) is necessary for them to warm their bodies, stimulate their appetites and digest their food.

Most dragons naturally regulate their own temperature by moving in and out of sunlight. This means that they need basking places in the warmth and light of the sun, and cooler, darker areas in which to withdraw. Full-sized earth and sky dragons in outdoor housing require ample sunny spaces as well as underground lairs (water dragons can either surface into sunlight or venture ashore). Artificial heating can control miniatures' indoor habitats; thermostats or thermometers are essential.

Light

Most dragons require 12–14 hours of ultraviolet light each day for enough vitamin D to maintain a healthy calcium level and prevent bone disease. What nature does not provide, you must. Natural sunlight is plentiful in outdoor enclosures. Windows and "full-spectrum" artificial light can supply indoor UV.

Housing Tip

Your dragon's immediate habitat is its home base, not a confinement. As soon as your dragon is trained, you can take it on walks and other outings, to the enjoyment of you both.

Indoor Habitats

If you selected a miniature dragon because you live in a typical house or apartment, space for your dragon's habitat is still a necessity. Your dragon needs a room of its own – not a cage or terrarium in the living room, nor a garage, or basement. Nor should it have the run of the house. It needs a comfortable, clean, controlled environment with sunny or well-lit areas for basking, and cool, dark places for hiding. Equipping the habitat will depend on whether you acquire your dragon as an egg or older creature, and whether it is an earth, sky, or water dragon.

Bathing and washing area

Shaded area

The habitat

- **Dragon Room** This should be spacious, as large as you have available. Like their full-sized counterparts, miniatures love to explore.
- **Materials** Substrates should be dragon-safe. No composition "hot rocks" containing heating elements. No wood chips or corn cob shavings. Tile is recommended.
- **Heat, light and air** The room should have controlled heat and cooling systems, artificial lighting, and adequate ventilation. (Bare light bulbs, oscillating fans and other dangerous accessories must be inaccessible to the dragon.)
- **Water** Running water is a must.
- **Ceiling** If you're acquiring a winged dragon, a high ceiling would be preferable.
- **Walls and floor** If you'll be raising a fire-breathing breed, you'll need fire-resistant covering on the floor and walls.
- **Bathroom** Your dragon will need an area to use as a bathroom. Paper towels on the floor will serve for most breeds; for fire-breathing dragons, fire-resistant litter will be necessary.

- **Decor** The room should be cheerful, with windows (skylights are optional) and shady corners. Hang colourful Impressionist art on the walls.
- **Storage** The room should have a cupboard for feed, collars and leashes, first aid kit and miscellaneous supplies.

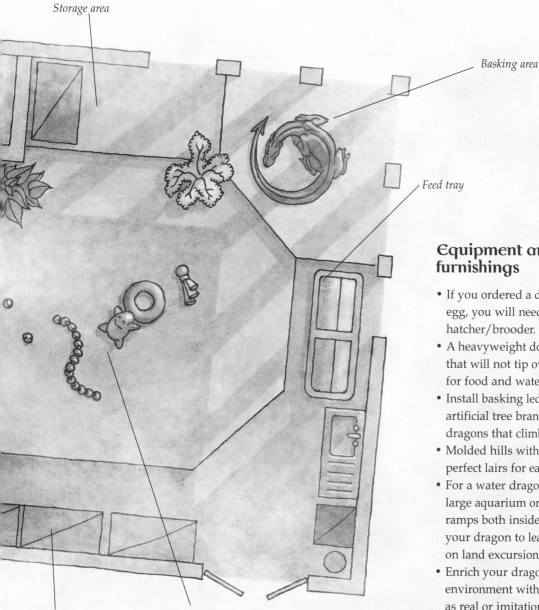

Storage area

Basking area

Feed tray

Storage area

Play area with toys

Equipment and furnishings

- If you ordered a dragon egg, you will need a hatcher/brooder.
- A heavyweight double feeder that will not tip over is best for food and water.
- Install basking ledges and/or artificial tree branches for dragons that climb.
- Molded hills with caves make perfect lairs for earth dragons.
- For a water dragon, provide a large aquarium or pool, with ramps both inside and out for your dragon to leave the water on land excursions.
- Enrich your dragon's environment with toys, such as real or imitation treasure for earth dragons, aquarium palaces for Asian Water Dragons, and sunken ships for Sea Dragons.
- Remember to purchase fireproof gloves for yourself if your dragon breathes fire.

The Dragon Room

Here is what a Dragon Room would look like if it were equipped for several breeds at the same time. You will probably prepare your dragon habitat for a single kind of animal, but should you actually want to raise more than one breed at a time, check with suppliers that the breeds and the sexes are compatible.

Outdoor Habitats
Earth dragons

Full-sized earth dragons require special – and expensive – housing. To raise one of these, you must have a hill on your property, with ample basking space. If the hillside does not already contain a spacious cave for a lair, you will have to provide one. Then there is the fencing, which will not only help keep your dragon home when the two of you are not together outside the enclosure, but will discourage human and animal intruders. For winged dragons, an aviary dome might be necessary. Those are the essentials. After them come food, water and the joys of raising a full-sized dragon.

Dragon Hill

Which breed of dragon will it be? Do you have a hillside spring flowing into a pool for a Drakon? A conical hill around which a Worm can coil and bask in the sun? A wooded hillside in which a Mountain Dragon of India can dream of elephants? A large hill sloping into enough open space to accommodate a Standard Western Dragon?

The lair

Whatever its breed, your earth dragon must have an underground lair. Unless there is already a cave in your hill, you'll need to construct one. That means contracting a crew with heavy equipment. (No one ever said preparing a home for a full-sized dragon was inexpensive. See my contractor's estimate, page 18.) Select an entrance location that faces a large basking area. Regardless of the current size of dragon you are acquiring, plan to make the lair large enough to accommodate the full-grown animal and its treasure. If you're unsure about its maximum potential size, consult your breeder. Structural bracing – as inconspicuous as possible – may be necessary to prevent a cave-in.

Enclosed area

Run water to this area. Place large food and watering troughs inside.

Fencing

A high stone or brick wall with a large gate would be effective for flightless dragons and would be perfect for a Mushussu. It would, however, cost a huge amount, and it would cut off your view of the dragon when you were outside the enclosure. Other options are a wooden or steel fence. Given that many dragons breathe fire, it would be unwise to build a wooden fence. Make certain the (usually locked) gate is large enough for your dragon to fit through when you go on your outings. If you have chosen to raise a winged animal, strong aviary mesh should cover the rest.

Water dragons

Does a river run through your property? Do you live on the shore of your own private lake? One of the two is essential if you have chosen to raise a full-sized water dragon. No Dragon Hill is necessary. For most water dragons, though, you will need to contract the building of an enclosure that will prevent your dragon from swimming outside your property or venturing beyond its designated space. Here are housing suggestions for full-sized water dragons:

River habitat

The Tarasque

Ancestors of this river monster enjoyed the expanse of the Rhône River; your river doesn't have to be that wide. Assuming local regulations permit, you will need to erect two sturdy fences across the river, as far apart as your property lines will allow. Steel posts should firmly secure the underwater fences between the river's banks. Because a Tarasque makes frequent land forays, fencing should also enclose the surrounding area.

The Piasa

Ideal housing for the winged Piasa also stretches across the river – not as a fence, but as an aviary enclosing a cliff overlooking turbulent water.

Lake habitat

Sea Dragons

Some varieties of freshwater Sea Dragons are amphibious (check with your supplier regarding the nature of your dragon) and therefore require fencing outside the shores of your lake. For such marine creatures, caves along a rocky shore make ideal homes. You will enjoy your dragon most if you join it in its domain. Rowing boats are recommended; motorboats, which can scar the animal, are not.

Asian Water Dragon

Because a shape-shifting Asian Water Dragon cannot be contained, fencing is useless. You can, though, entice one of the breed to live in your lake by providing it with an opulent underwater palace. To visit the Dragon King in its domain, you'll need diving gear – but don't be surprised if the dragon appears in human form, as is the habit of that breed.

If constructing such an enclosure is too costly and challenging for you or local contractors, there is another way to attract an Asian Water Dragon to your lake (see pages 102–103).

Equipment and Supplies

Don't think that your preparations are complete once the housing for a full-sized dragon is in place. An outbuilding adjoining the enclosure for a full-sized dragon is necessary for the storage of everything you need to raise and care for your animal. Equipment and supplies will vary according to the dragon's stage of growth and its breed.

The outbuilding

The storage shed should be spacious – large enough for you to work in comfortably. The building will be part of the enclosure, with posts attached to the facing corners of the structure. One of the shed's two doors allows you access from outside; the other opens into the enclosure. If you are raising a fire-breathing dragon, the roof and walls of the building must be fire-resistant.

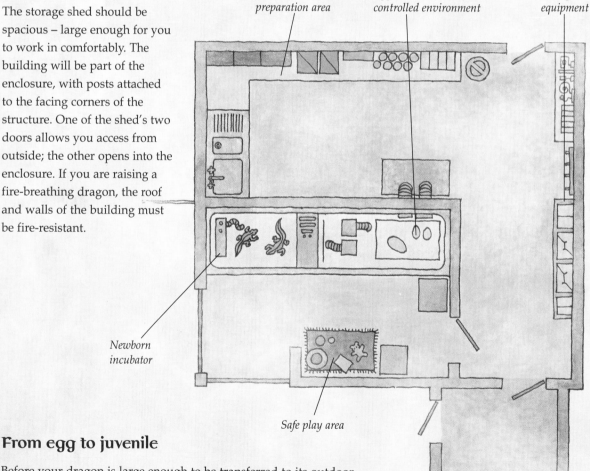

Washing and feed preparation area

Eggs are monitored in a controlled environment

Storage and equipment

Newborn incubator

Safe play area

From egg to juvenile

Before your dragon is large enough to be transferred to its outdoor enclosure, your storage area will be your Dragon Room, equipped with a hatcher/brooder, terrarium, food, cleaning and medical supplies, soft toys and so on (see pages 66–67).

Adult dragon provisions

If your dragon is already an adult – or if you are preparing
for its maturation – the following should be among the
equipment and supplies stored in your outbuilding:

*Long hose for washing your dragon; strong
detergent; brushes with and without handles;
a barrel of polish; and boxes of cloths*

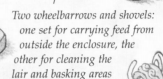

*Two wheelbarrows and shovels:
one set for carrying feed from
outside the enclosure, the
other for cleaning the
lair and basking areas*

*Fire-extinguishing
equipment for small
grass fires*

*Tinsnips or metal shears
for trimming claws*

*Medical supplies,
including large
bottles of peroxide
and metre-wide rolls
of gauze for cuts and
scrapes, and a tub of calcium
tablets with vitamin D*

*Tack area
containing gear for
training and riding*

*Chest of
treasure
and toys*

*Ultraviolet heating lamps with long
extension cords for cold days*

*If needed, a fireproof
suit for you*

*CD player and outside speakers for whatever
kind of music pleases your dragon*

My Dragon Village

Here are sketches of my property, made after I installed fencing and built the storage shed. Your enclosure may well look like this, ready for the arrival of your dragon. I've made notes on the pictures to point out housing features for different breeds.

Dragon Hill

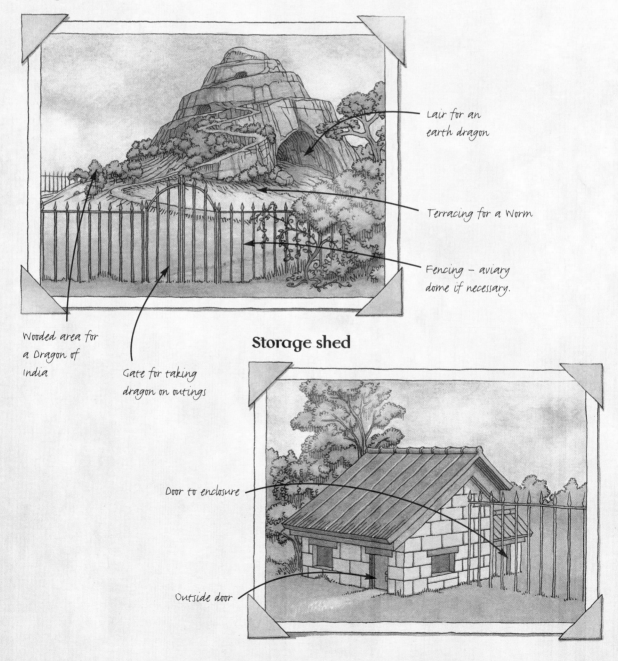

Lair for an earth dragon

Terracing for a Worm

Fencing – aviary dome if necessary.

Wooded area for a Dragon of India

Gate for taking dragon on outings

Storage shed

Door to enclosure

Outside door

River housing

Cliff for a Piasa (aviary dome not pictured)

Fencing

River home of a Tarasque

Lake housing

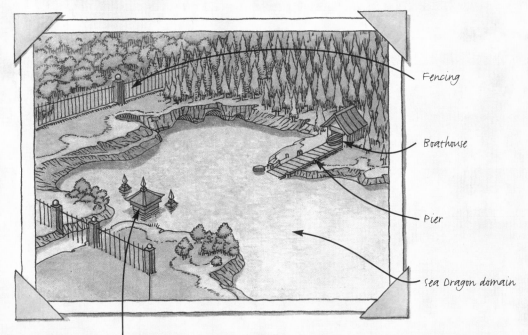

Fencing

Boathouse

Pier

Sea Dragon domain

Dragon King's palace (underwater)

Your Dragon Comes Home!

Inform your supplier that all housing preparations have been made. If you ordered an egg, it will be sent directly to you. Suppliers ship water dragons in special tanks, but an earth dragon can either be shipped to you or you can pick it up personally and accompany it to its new home. In case you choose the latter option, here are some guidelines for transporting your dragon.

Accompanying a small dragon

There are two major methods for transporting a dragon egg, small juvenile, or miniature.

By vehicle

If you live in the same country or continent as the supplier, and your dragon is a juvenile, you can transport it by car, van or lorry. (Even if distance and size of the dragon are no issue, transport of the animal in a bicycle basket or motorcycle sidecar is considered unsafe and is not recommended.) Remember, though, not to place your young dragon in the boot of a car, which lacks ventilation and can fill with poisonous exhaust fumes. Regardless of the size of your vehicle, secure the crate with seat belts, in a back seat if possible.

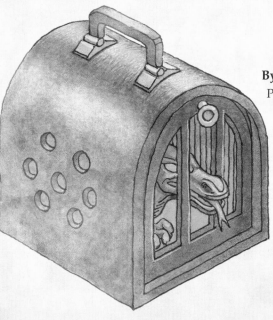

By air

Passenger airlines accept animal carriers up to a certain size. (A carrier for a small dragon will even fit under your seat.) But when you carry or wheel the cage through airports, people who peek inside will be surprised.

Accompanying a large dragon

Depending on the distance and locations, a full-sized adult dragon can be transported by several different methods – or a combination thereof.

By air
The dragon would have to be transported by cargo plane.

By water
A leisurely ocean voyage would be relaxing for you following months of housing construction. As you sat on deck, it would be pleasant to think of the ship as an ark with a special cargo.

By rail
Your dragon would be considered too dangerous to the other animals to be permitted passage on a cattle train. You might book your dragon more easily on a circus-owned carrier or a coal truck.

By road
A rented semi-trailer would suffice. The dragon's hissing or roaring, however, could be disconcerting to lorry-park patrons.

Hatching a Dragon Egg

A mother dragon in the wild typically built a nest of decaying vegetation, which produced heat as it decomposed. After she laid the eggs, the mother dragon covered them with materials from the nest and patiently watched over her eggs for the many weeks before they hatched. Often, she would curl around the mounded nest to protect her natural treasure from intruders. As the surrogate mother, a dragon raiser who begins with an egg must reproduce the conditions for a successful hatching.

Preliminary care of the egg

Candling

Once you have determined from the shape and colouring of the egg that the supplier has shipped you the dragon breed you ordered, candle the egg to confirm that it contains a single yolk. With a powerful light, you should be able to see the little dragon heart beating. If it is not, return the egg to the supplier, demanding a replacement.

Storage

The egg is dormant before incubation begins. Store it in a cool, dry place, out of sunlight (55°F, 12°C is ideal) for up to six days after you receive it. The longer the egg is stored, the longer it will take to hatch.

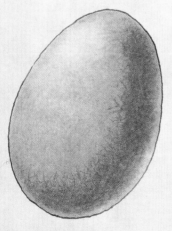

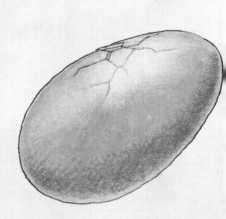

0–4 hours   *5–8 hours*   *9–12 hours*

Incubators

Necessary features

Like the incubation equipment for other animals, a dragon hatcher/brooder needs reliable control of air flow, temperature (99.5°F, 37.5°C), and humidity. I recommend the clear-view variety, which allows you to watch the hatching action. Incubation times vary for different breeds. Check with your supplier.

Note: *Since the Asian Dragon remains in the shell for up to three thousand years, it's critical that before the egg is put on the market, the supplier determine its age and that the young is ready to hatch. Also, large Asian Dragons should be hatched out-of-doors because they immediately grow to full size.*

Size

The size of hatcher/brooder you need depends first of all on whether you purchased the egg of a miniature or a full-sized dragon. Eggs of miniature dragons tend to be the size of goose eggs, while those of larger animals approximate the 9 x 12-inch (22.5 x 30-cm) *Aepyornis maximus*, the famous fossilized egg of the Elephant Bird of Madagascar.

You'll be thrilled when you see the egg begin to crack and the first tiny dragon tongue or claw curve out of the shell. It will take up to 24 hours for the shiny baby dragon to work its way out of the egg.

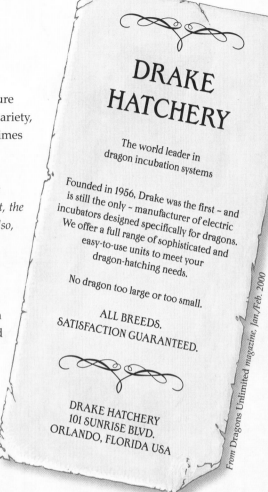

DRAKE HATCHERY

The world leader in dragon incubation systems

Founded in 1956, Drake was the first – and is still the only – manufacturer of electric incubators designed specifically for dragons. We offer a full range of sophisticated and easy-to-use units to meet your dragon-hatching needs.

No dragon too large or too small.

ALL BREEDS. SATISFACTION GUARANTEED.

DRAKE HATCHERY
101 SUNRISE BLVD.
ORLANDO, FLORIDA USA

From Dragons Unlimited magazine, Jan./Feb. 2000

13–16 hours   *17–20 hours*   *21–24 hours*

Communication

Now that your dragon is in its new home, it's up to you to initiate communication and learn your dragon's body language. Only through mutual understanding and respect will the two of you have the full, satisfying and lasting relationship that you desire and it deserves.

Introducing yourself

Here are the initial steps in interacting with your dragon:

- Every time you approach your dragon, you send it signals about you and how you will relate to it. Even a hatchling, like a newborn human, will begin to bond with its dragon-raiser "parent". It will immediately accept its surroundings, feeding patterns and your presence. You must, in turn, take into account its breed, latent temperament and its emerging personality. The older the dragon, the longer it will take for the two of you to get to know and trust each other.

- As soon as it is able to move around, your dragon will begin exploring. You should be present so that it will understand that you are part of its new environment.

Dragon body language

Physical expression can reveal what your dragon is feeling or thinking. Be careful, though – a single signal can mean more than one thing. Familiarity with the dragon will help you interpret.

Contraction or dilation of the pupils
I'm irritated – or excited – or thinking.

Head on your shoulder
(No explanation needed.)

Head bobbing
I realize you are there – or this is my territory. (While this action may seem to be a greeting, it is usually an assertion of superiority and a warning to keep one's distance.)

*My Rowena is partial
to the guitar.*

• Spend as much time as you can with your dragon during its
first weeks with you. Offer to feed a young dragon by hand
and fill food and water troughs while an older
dragon watches. Address your dragon by
name and speak to it softly so that it
comes to recognize your voice. Humming
is also effective, particularly with hatchlings.
Read aloud to your dragon (no dragon-slayer
tales allowed). Play soothing recorded music
such as string quartets and compositions for harp, lute,
or classical guitar. If you play these instruments yourself,
that's even better.

Open mouth
*I'm overheated – or yawning.
(Rowena will sometimes yawn
when I do, imitating me.)*

Closing of eyes
*I'm content – or don't want
company – or am asleep.*

Fire-breathing
*I am stressed – or angry –
or I just feel like it.*

Feeding

Dragons are primarily carnivores. The beasts of old were notorious for devouring prey – horns, hoofs, hide, backbone and all. (It's said that dragon waste sometimes contained even twisted body armour or a crushed helmet.) It's impractical, though, for a dragon raiser to stock live food such as sheep, cattle, or horses in quantities sufficient for a dragon's appetite. Modern breeds – both young and adult – require modern forms of food, all fortified with calcium and vitamin D.

Hatchlings

While hatchlings are by nature as carnivorous as older dragons, they eat a variety of rations.

First, don't plan on saving your dragon's eggshell as a souvenir. It will be the first food the hatchling eats after its emergence from the egg. After that, here are my own recipes for feed that will nourish and please most newly-hatched Western and Asian Dragons. Begin with small portions and serve your young dragon ever greater quantities with decreasing frequency as it grows.

The following recipes are for hatchlings of full-size dragons. For miniatures, reduce the original amounts to one tablespoon. In both cases, quadruple the quantities with each decrease in frequency.

Baby Dragon Chow (Western)

50 ml milk

30 g crumbled honey cake

Calcium/vitamin D supplement

Mix and serve.

Baby Dragon Chow (Asian)

50 ml cream

30 g ground bamboo shoots

Calcium/vitamin D supplement

Mix and serve.

Feeding Frequency

1–2 months – four times daily

3–4 months – three times daily

5–6 months – twice daily

After 6 months – adult fare

Adult earth dragons

For earth dragons of all sizes larger than hatchlings, I would recommend All-Purpose Dragon Chow. You can order it from your supplier in either dry or moist form. Both varieties are delivered in barrels by lorry. Feeding amount and frequency will vary according to the size, breed and needs of your dragon. Here is information from the label of the moist variety:

INGREDIENTS:
OXEN BY-PRODUCT, GUAR GUM, POTASSIUM CHLORIDE, HYDROLYZED SOYA PROTEIN, SODIUM TRIPOLYPHOSPHATE, SPRING WATER, YEAST EXTRACT, SALT, PEPPER, BEEF BY-PRODUCT, NATURAL FLAVOURS, ELEPHANT BY-PRODUCT, CARRAGEENAN, ZINC SULFATE, PEARLS, THIAMINE MONONITRATE, BAY LEAVES, CURRY, COPPER SULFATE, BRONZE, HONEY, LAMB BY-PRODUCT, CALCIUM AND VITAMIN D SUPPLEMENTS, GOLD, SAFFRON, NIACIN, BIOTIN, CARAMEL COLOUR, GARLIC, IRON, CRICKET BY-PRODUCTS, RIBOFLAVIN.

Housetraining

What goes in comes out in a different form. Juvenile earth dragons need to be trained to use a litter tray. Earth dragons acquired as adults will already have been taught to withdraw to a single area.

Adult water dragons

A full-sized Sea Dragon in your private lake will eat fish and seaweed; the mysterious Asian Water Dragon fends for itself; both the amphibious Tarasque and the cliff-dwelling Piasa need prepared meat on land. Food for miniatures of these is small portions of the same, including fish food for the aquarium dragons.

Health and Grooming

Dragon raisers from around the world have written to me about dragon health and grooming. Here are some frequently asked questions.

Health

Q Do I need to exercise my dragon?

A Of course. Once your miniature or full-sized earth dragon has undergone standard training, take it on daily outings – for its health, and yours as well. Besides, walks are enjoyable and will help you two to relate emotionally.

Q What's the most common health problem that dragons have?

A Metabolic bone disease (MBD). A deficiency of calcium can result in "rubber jaw", a softening of the jawbone, and a weakening of bones in the feet. This process can be reversed by supplementing the diet with calcium and vitamin D and increasing the animal's exposure to ultraviolet (UV) light.

Q How do I know if my dragon is sick?

A I recommend keeping a daily health record of your dragon's habits and appearance. Entries will indicate changes in eating and sleeping, energy level, the colour of scales and the colour and consistency of dragon waste. If these changes continue, look for a qualified veterinary surgeon.

Q How do I go about choosing a trustworthy veterinary surgeon for my dragon?

A Dog and cat hospitals are everywhere, and every rural area has a large-animal vet who works with cattle and horses. Unfortunately, I've never seen a veterinary surgeon ad in Dragons Unlimited magazine. Nor have I ever heard about any vet who specializes in the treatment of dragons. An animal doctor who provides reptile care would be the next best choice – although it's unlikely that you'll find such a specialist in your vicinity. Talk to your local vet and decide if you would be comfortable taking your young or miniature dragon to him or her, or arranging a home visit for a full-sized dragon.

Author's Note
I once talked to one of our local vets, Dr Gordie Miller, about dragon health. "Same as for you and me," he said. "Sensible diet, exercise, and . . ." – a hint of a self-satisfied grin – "no smoking." I never approached him again.

Q Can I contract salmonella from my dragon?

A Yes, dragons can be carriers of salmonella bacteria. Practise good personal hygiene by washing your hands with warm, soapy water before and after physical contact with your dragon.

Q I've heard of "mouth rot". Does it have anything to do with fire-breathing?

A Not at all. Mouth rot is an infection evidenced by a crusty spot around the dragon's mouth. It should be treated immediately with a topical antibiotic. If untreated, it will spread and could be fatal.

Q My dragon has ticks in his ears. How do I get rid of them?

A The same as you would remove the parasites from any other animal: with tweezers or forceps. Then rub the area with alcohol.

Grooming

Q How do you bathe a dragon?

Q Should I have a veterinary declaw my hatchling or clip its wings to make it less dangerous when it grows larger?

A Absolutely not. Such limiting of a dragon's powers is, first, cruel to the animal and, second, makes it less valuable for renting out or showing.

A *Carefully. Do not suddenly grasp an earth hatchling and dip it into a basin. You could frighten it for life, and it would claw and bite you, breathe fire if it is able, and thrash you with its tail. Only after weeks or months of building your dragon's trust with gentle handling should you wash it for the first time – and even then you must proceed gradually.*

Begin by brushing it with a soft cloth dampened with warm water. After repeated washings of this kind, introduce it to the basin. Holding the hatchling in your hand, lower it into the water more each day. Never use soap. (Soap in the eyes, like sudden immersion, would panic your dragon.) Then wrap the hatchling in a soft, dry towel – and it will welcome the bathing experience thereafter.

Washing a full-sized earth dragon is another matter. Again, you must gain its trust over time. Perhaps one day when it is drinking at the trough you can dip a towel into the water and rub it over a shoulder, then onto the body. If you are careful (and you don't want to incite your dragon's ire), you'll eventually be able to wash the animal with a hose and a long-handled brush.

Q Should I polish my dragon's scales?

A You can – if your dragon lets you. But keep in mind that enhancing the natural gloss of scales is more for the benefit of human onlookers (e.g., show judges) than it is for the well-being of the dragon. For full-sized dragons, you might need a stepladder.

Q Is it necessary to trim a dragon's claws – and if so, how do you do it?

A The claws of dragons in the wild were as nature intended. For their own safety, though, dragon raisers are advised to dull the needle-sharp points. The sensitive process, like dragon bathing, requires your dragon's trust over an extended period of time. For young and miniature dragons, use special reptile claw clippers; for full-sized dragons, use tinsnips. In either case, trim minimally. Take care not to cut the quick, which would cause bleeding – and rage.

part 4
Training Your Dragon

Your dragon has by now grown accustomed to you and its environment, and you have been observing its personality and abilities. It's time to begin training it for activities that will satisfy – even fulfill – both of you. As communication between the two of you develops, you'll discover that you and your dragon have actually been "training" each other for your years together.

Training Begins

Is your dragon a miniature, juvenile, or larger animal? Does it have two legs, four, even six – or none at all? Does it have wings? More than one head? Is it an earth dragon or water dragon? Is it Western or Asian? The size and breed of the animal will determine what equipment and techniques are needed for training. For the sake of simplicity and consideration of book length, let's assume that you wish to train a Western earth dragon. What follows can be adapted to the training needs of other kinds of dragons.

Preparation

Step 1

Having gained your dragon's trust over months of interacting and communicating with it, measure your animal – the neck diameter for a miniature or juvenile dragon, the head for a full-grown beast. This does, of course, require great care. If you frighten your animal, you might be bitten or burned, and you might not regain its trust for many months – not to mention your own time in the hospital!

Step 2

Taking care to specify the breed, name, age and size of your dragon, order appropriate training equipment from your supplier. These items are specially designed for dragons. Collars and halters, for example, are made of fine chain mail for strength and durability and covered with velvet to prevent injury to delicate scales. Leashes and leads are made of woven wire with a high tensile strength.

Step 3

After your equipment arrives, begin the training phase of your lives together by sitting down beside your dragon and addressing it by name. Keeping eye contact all the while, tell it how necessary "working together" (training) is for doing any number of things the two of you would enjoy, from taking walks together outside its enclosure to competing in dragon shows. The dragon will not necessarily understand what you are saying, but your body language and the sound of your words will reassure it of your friendship. Offer it some honey cake, a traditional dragon favourite. Dragons are not above subtle bribery with treats.

Author's Note
I don't like the term "obedience training" when it comes to dragons. If you have established rapport with your miniature or young dragon over a period of months, it will welcome new experiences with you. You will have a better life with your dragon if you think of training in terms of giving it opportunities to engage in different activities.

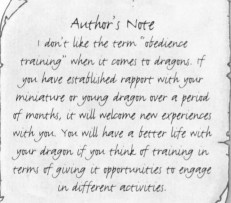

Step 4

Show your dragon its equipment and allow the animal to inspect it, being careful not to subject the velvet to a burst of flame. Carefully, slowly, speaking softly all the while, fit your dragon with its first piece of equipment: a collar for a small dragon, a halter for a large one.

Training — Small Dragons

You have passed the milestone of fitting your miniature or small dragon with a collar. Allow a week for the animal to become accustomed to this new part of its life before you progress to the next training step: attaching a leash. This is the beginning of the slow process necessary in preparing your dragon for further training and, ultimately, for competing in dragon shows.

"Come"

Carry the leash into the Dragon Room or outdoor enclosure with you and place it on the floor or ground. Sit down beside your dragon and address it by name. The animal will naturally be curious about what you brought into its habitat. As you softly repeat your dragon's name, it will, in time (be patient, no matter how long it takes), cautiously approach the strange object and examine it. Touch your dragon gently, whisper, or hum. Hold up the end of the leash, and taking care not to frighten the dragon, clip the end to the collar. Reward it with a honey-cake treat.

Walking with a leash

Again, in time, the dragon will drag the leash around its area. Follow it and eventually pick up the free end and continue following your animal.

"Heel"

Consistently repeat the leash procedure over a period of days before drawing your dragon closer to you. Then, move your free hand lower on the leash until the two of you are walking side by side. Accompany the action with the "Heel" command. On following days, change walking direction, to the left and to the right.

"Sit"/"Stay"

Replace the leash with the expandable variety. After the two of you have been walking together for many minutes, stop. Step in front of the animal, and, as you give the oral command to sit, gently press down on its hindquarters. Once it is sitting, hold one hand palm forwards and tell it to stay. With hand still upheld, back away slowly, as far as the leash will reach, then return to the animal. Another treat is in order after a successful instance. Repeat the process day after day.

"Fly!"

If you have a winged dragon that has not yet tested its wings, slowly lift the attached leash above its head and give the "Fly" command. The wings will begin to flap. As you turn, lifting the leash higher, the dragon will rise into the air and circle higher around you until you whistle like a falconer, lower the leash, and return the animal to a sitting position. In time, when the dragon is ready, dispense with the leash.

Leaving the enclosure

When you feel the time is right, begin taking your dragon out of its habitat – eventually without a leash.

Training — Large Dragons

It should come as no surprise that training a large dragon is different from training a small one. Size and corresponding strength determine what the animal can – or can't – do. What a large dragon does is, finally, its choice – not the dragon raiser's. Be alert to body language indicating displeasure. If your dragon does not follow your training guidance, attempt to make it understand the activity. If the dragon decides it is something it would enjoy, it will join forces with you.

Leading

"Leading" is actually a misnomer. If the dragon is interested in participating, the two of you will be able to take long, leisurely walks together.

After your dragon has become accustomed to the halter, cautiously attach the lead line. Hold the line loosely, with "good hands", 6–8 inches (15–20 cm) below the clip. For safety's sake, stand about a foot (30 cm) away from your dragon's left shoulder as you do this. Talking softly all the while, slowly move forwards until it is moving with you. Walk with it around the enclosure, matching its stride to avoid being stepped on. Follow the leading procedure daily for weeks.

After you have repeatedly walked with your dragon in its habitat and are confident of its actions, venture with it outside, beginning with a stroll around the outside of its enclosure and increasing the distance of your outing each time. You can eventually dispense with the lead line altogether and you two can enjoy long afternoons in the hills or beside a shady river. Take along food for two and a book to read aloud.

Collar

Line driving

Line driving can prepare your dragon to pull your personal cart around your property or participate in chariot events at dragon shows.

First, you will need the help of an assistant through every early stage of the training. Measure the girth, shoulders, and head of your dragon so you can order a harness from a supplier. After harnessing your dragon for the first time, attach long lines to the bit and run them through harness loops. Then, while your assistant leads, walk along behind, holding the reins, getting a feel for turning your dragon as you circle inside the enclosure.

The day will come when you attach your light, two-wheeled cart or chariot to your dragon and the two of you can explore deserted country roads or compete in shows.

Ancient chariots

Western Dragons pulled the chariot of the witch Medea through the air, and Eastern Dragons drew the two-wheeled carriages of Chinese emperors through clouds and waves.

Back band

Rein

Cart or chariot shaft

Riding — Earth Dragons

Here is where people who choose to raise miniature dragons lose out. After a large dragon reaches full growth (at about three years), it is ready to be ridden. Riding requires long-term training for both dragon and rider, but it is truly one of the joys of dragon raising. Different breeds require different saddle and tack, present different challenges, and reward you with different adventures.

Breeds and equipment

Some dragon breeds are more physically and temperamentally suited for riding than others. The ease or difficulty of training and riding your dragon will depend on which breed you choose to raise.

Here are a few breeds representing the range of tack, gear and riding challenges facing dragon raisers. These samples will give you some idea of the specialized equipment and skills you will need to ride your dragon.

Conventional bit and bridle

Long reins (because of the animal's long neck)

Light riding saddle

Stirrups

Mushussu (Sirrush)

The long-legged and straight-backed consort of Babylonian gods is the most equine in build and the fastest runner of all the breeds. Accustomed to serving a god, it is easily trained. Due to its long neck, though, the animal's head is at or above the rider's eye level, making it difficult for the rider to see.

Heavily padded saddle

Velvet lining

Wide reins

Stirrups

Standard Western Dragon

The plated ridge down this dragon's back requires a specially-designed saddle, heavily padded and lined with velvet. The reins of fire-breathing varieties should be wide and fire-resistant. This breed is a more stable mount than the two-legged Wyvern.

Howdah

Reins

Muzzle

Easily detachable belly band

Training

The more experience you have had with horsemanship the better. If you've had none, lessons are in order. Once the special tack and gear arrives from your supplier, adapt the standard horse-training process to your breed of dragon.

Bridling This is an easy task with all but Multiheaded Dragons.

Saddling Let the dragon become used to the saddle before mounting.

Mounting Extreme nervousness is natural the first time in the saddle.

Trotting, cantering, galloping Attempt whatever gaits your animal (and your nerves) are capable of.

Riding in the open Eventually, you and your dragon will be ready to venture outside the enclosure.

Tarasque

The spiked shell of the six-legged Tarasque posed a distinct problem for saddle-makers. They met the challenge by devising a howdah that would fit onto the animal's back. (The equipment is detachable in the event that the amphibious Tarasque enters water.) The lion's head of the beast requires a muzzle instead of a bit and bridle.

Riding — Water Dragons

Dragon raisers who acquire a breed of water dragon are, themselves, an unusual breed. They love the smell and changing moods of bodies of water. They revel in boating, swimming and diving into dark depths shafted with light. They have a private lake on their property and the financial resources to invest in additional expenses for the sake of a marine creature and the unique pleasures it provides. And finally, they know that they do not actually raise or train a water dragon as much as they offer the creature a habitat in which it can thrive.

Sea Dragons

The dragon raiser must mount the Sea Dragon without saddle and reins. But how can you get close to a Sea Dragon in the first place? And what happens to you when it dives beneath the surface?

Approaching a Sea Dragon

It is easier to calculate the girth of a Sea Dragon than it is to fit it with tack and gear. For this reason, no suppliers offer riding equipment for varieties of this breed. This is why you must be able to ride without benefit of such supplies. Here are some suggestions for realizing your dream:

• Sea Dragons are often most active at night. On a night when the moon is full, load your sailing boat or rowing boat with buckets of fresh fish.

• From a hillside above the lake, scan the waters with a pair of strong binoculars. You may have to do this for hours or days before you locate the dragon.

• When it surfaces, sail or row out to where you last saw it and empty a bucket of fish into the water.

• Repeat the feeding until the dragon rises to the surface.

• Drift beside the animal as it moves, getting it accustomed to your presence. Sing to it.

• On a subsequent night, again venture out to the Sea Dragon – again with food – but this time, drop anchor and swim with the dragon.

• When you feel the time is right, crawl up onto the dragon's back and ride through the night. When it dives, take a deep breath and hold on.

Dragon, My Darlin'

My favourite sea
Dragon song

Asian Water Dragons

As I've said before, varieties of the Asian Dragon are the most difficult to interact with. You can never hope to raise them or train them – even from eggs that hatch after three thousand years, because the hatchlings immediately grow to full size. And thereafter, they change size and shape at will. The best anyone can do is attract them with something that captivates their interest. In the case of Asian Water Dragons, build it and they will come.

Imperial dragon boat

One way to draw an Asian Dragon to your private lake is to construct a two- or three-story deckhouse worthy of an emperor, with dragon-head decorations projecting from the peaks of the tile roofs. The conception for this boat derives from the ancient story of a Chinese monk who fell in love with a Korean girl. When he left her to return to his native China, she transformed herself into a dragon and carried his boat on her back through stormy seas.

On these pages is the picture of a deckhouse for an imperial dragon boat. Your selected carpenter can use this as the starting place for drawing a blueprint. Notice that beneath the deck, the bottom of the structure is an inverted "V", designed to fit upon the back of an Asian Dragon interested in resurrecting the glories of the past. You needn't be concerned about the size of the deckhouse because the dragon can change its size accordingly. The size of the boat is limited by your finances.

Once your completed deckhouse – brightly painted, with pennants fluttering – floats upon your lake, you will wait eagerly for the arrival of your dragon. One fine day the dragon will be there, waiting for you. You'll cross the gangplank and your dragon-powered boat will disembark.

Dragon-boat races

A dragon boat that is far more affordable
than the imperial variety is the kind entered
in dragon-boat races. It is, though, different
from the 40-foot (12-m) boats that
participate in the popular racing events held
worldwide. Those have detachable prows
and sterns representing dragon heads and
tails, and twenty paddlers man the craft. In
authentic races, passengers sit on seats fitted
on the backs of actual swimming dragons.

Viking Dragon Ships

Warships of the Norsemen bore prows carved in the shapes
of dragon heads and coiling sterns resembling serpent tails.
These long, narrow craft, floating on the waves or virtually
flying under full sail, embodied the elemental forces of the
dragon family.

Riding – Sky Dragons

The terrors and joys of flight can be yours if your companion is a winged Western Dragon or if you can lure an Asian Dragon to your property. You will need to order special equipment from your supplier and reserve air space from your area's air traffic controller. In any case, be sure to carry your personal information on you in case of mishap.

Western winged dragons

Of the two major breeds of flying dragons, the Western and the Asian, the Western is by far the easier and the safer to ride. It lives on your property, is trainable, and you can choose different riding methods and equipment.

Training

Preparation for flight on a winged Western Dragon begins with the same leading and line-driving training as that of wingless dragons (see pages 96–97).

The next stage is aerial training with a harness and 40-foot (12-m) line of woven wire. To strengthen the dragon's wings, stand in the centre of the enclosure, holding one end of the line as the dragon circles above you. Train it to land at a falconer's whistle. (For similar training involving winged miniatures, see page 95.) This exercise establishes the eventual free-flight point of departure and return.

Equipment

You can choose from at least three modes of travel on a winged Western Dragon:

• **Saddle and harness** This is the most conventional method. The rider, like a jet fighter pilot or racing car driver, straps himself or herself into a harness. This is attached to a special saddle upon the dragon's back, in front of the wings. Steering

"Dragons"

If your flying dragon breathes fire in the night sky, gazers on the ground might think they are seeing a shooting star. But this flame comes from a real dragon – unlike the celestial glow that people in the Middle Ages called "dragons" and thought were serpents in the sky.

is done not with a wheel but with reins. If the driver loses grip on the reins, the dragon will, in any case, eventually circle back to its landing site.

- **Gondola** Less frightening – but also less exhilarating – than riding on the dragon's back is sitting in a balloon basket beneath its belly. As is true with hot-air balloons, landing is the most problematic part of the flight. The rider simply must trust the dragon to return to earth safely.

Note: *Due to the danger of landing, choose the gondola method of flight only with a two-legged Wyvern. A four-legged dragon would crush both the basket and you.*

- **The Sinbad method** This is the most fundamental and economical of all dragon-flight techniques. Just as Sinbad the Sailor used his turban to tie himself to the leg of the giant *Rukh* (Roc), the dragon rider attaches a specially made harness to the dragon's rear left leg.

Enjoy!

Regardless of the gear selected to become airborne, the dragon rider will look down with amazement as his or her property shrinks below and the world spreads out in all directions.

Asian Sky Dragons

Since you cannot raise an Asian Dragon, how can you attract one for a dragon flight? There are ways, just as there are kinds of equipment suited for aerial adventure with such a dragon.

Appealing to a Sky Dragon

Perhaps an Asian Water Dragon already lives in your private lake and is part of the imperial dragon boat or participates in dragon-boat races. It just might be that this dragon flies aloft on stormy nights or chases its Cosmic Pearl among the clouds when the moon is full.

Observe the dragon night after night, and if it rises into the sky, present yourself to it when it returns. Offer it a basketful of roasted swallows and show it your riding equipment (see Riding Tip, opposite). Speak to it gently, and gesture with your hands that you would like to journey with it in the air. You might need to repeat your overtures many times before it welcomes your company prior to a flight.

On the other hand, a sky dragon might be drawn to your property because another dragon of its family already dwells there. In this case, follow the enticements outlined above.

If you have no private lake, go out into the open on a night of scudding clouds. Place a basket of roasted swallows at your feet and bang copper pans together in a clanging signal to dragons aloft. If a sky dragon is in the area, it might be curious and investigate the sound. Once again, present your case for flight.

Equipment

In fanciful art, animals or human figures simply sit astride the backs of Asian Dragons swirling through the sky. You, though, will need equipment – a saddle and harness similar to that used on winged Western Dragons. Asian Dragon tack, though, accommodates a narrower dragon body with a lower back ridge. Since you cannot measure your dragon beforehand, you will have to trust your supplier to know the approximate size of such a dragon.

Riding Tip

For possible inclement weather aloft, helmet, goggles and rain gear are a must for Asian Sky Dragon riders. This is the equipment I used on that memorable stormy ride that was wilder than any in an amusement park.

part 5
Presenting Your Dragon

By now, you and your dragon have been with each other day in and day out, trained together, enjoyed excursions together and shared adventures. If both of you are willing, you two are ready to go public. You can engage in a variety of business pursuits, or you can participate in public events and dragon shows. Opportunities beckon for presenting your dragon to the world at large.

Renting Out Your Dragon

There are many opportunities to rent out a willing dragon: to guard property, appear at public events, serve as a model for dragon art and a host of others. Of these, modelling is not only the most lucrative, it is also particularly satisfying for both dragon raiser and dragon. The dragon raiser is given images and objects to display throughout his or her dwelling, and the dragon is pleased to represent its kind to both the elite and the public at large.

Heraldry

Heraldic artists who are commissioned to create coats of arms for some of the most highly respected families and institutions on earth are always looking for distinguished sources for their art. There is no better heraldic model than an actual animal – in our case, a dragon.

Dragons have a long history as graphic symbols of strength, courage and vigilance. Use of the dragon in British heraldry hearkens back to emblems on shields and banners and the dragon-shaped windsocks of Roman armies. Uther Pendragon ("pendragon" meaning head dragon or chieftan) adopted the figure and passed the image

Statant
(Standing)

Passant
(Walking)

on to his son, Arthur. From the time of the Norman Conquest, the dragon dominated the flags and pennants of British kings. It afterwards entered heraldry as a supporter of Tudor royal arms and became the Red Dragon of Wales.

The dragon of British heraldry has four legs and the ribbed wings of a bat. Its tongue and tail are barbed. Continental European coats of arms, on the other hand, render the dragon as a two-legged Wyvern with a *nowed* (knotted) tail.

If your dragon matches either of these forms, it would make a perfect model for a coat of arms. Depicted as a Wyvern with the head of a cock instead of a dragon, the Cockatrice is also a heraldic *charge* (symbol). And a Multiheaded Dragon occasionally appears in crests. But those breeds are so difficult to work with that there would be little demand for their services.

Let's assume that your dragon is suited for a coat of arms. To prepare the animal to be depicted graphically and described verbally in blazon by a herald, you will need to instruct it in the stances of heraldic dragons: *statant* (standing), *passant* (walking), *rampant* (rearing up), and *volant* (flying).

**Rampant
(Rearing up)**

**Volant
(Flying)**

Gift catalogues

The retail world – and the public – is hungry for dragons. Untold thousands of the creature in all imaginable forms and materials populate gift shops and mail-order catalogues worldwide. The greatest demand is for representations of the four-legged Western Dragon and the two-legged Wyvern, or the serpentine Asian Dragon. So, if your dragon is of a standard variety, and the novelty of modelling for commercial art appeals to both of you, it shouldn't be difficult to find an artist who would like to design items based on an actual dragon. It could be fun for all.

The host of dragon creations already available includes dragon sculpture, figurines, jewellery, china, vases, sword hilts, wall hangings, mirrors, sconces, candleholders, fireplace andirons, rugs, fountains, letter openers, music boxes, ashtrays, posters, T-shirts, incense burners, coasters, tattoos, stickers, you name it. Here are a couple of pages from *Dragonlogue*, a mail-order catalogue of dragon merchandise.

Home Decor

Handsome dragon accents will decorate your home from top to bottom.

BOOK GUARDIANS
Your treasured volumes will be safe under the watchful eyes of these two vigilant dragons. Minutely detailed, these famed keepers of their own golden hoards will discourage any unwanted borrowers. Made of stone-textured resin composite. Weighted bases with felt covering. Each bookend 9 in (23 cm) high.

SKY DRAGON WEATHERVANE
Asian Dragons are traditionally renowned as weather-lords, rulers of clouds, wind and rain. The dragon atop this copper weathervane will tell you what is happening in the sky so that you can plan your day accordingly. Spindle and dragon 36 in (91 cm) high; arrow 24 in (61 cm) long.

FLYING COLOURS

You needn't be afraid of these flying dragons. They will brighten up your windows with their flight. Entirely hand-crafted glass collectibles. Each comes with a looped golden thread. Set of two. 5 in (13 cm) high.

IMPERIAL COMFORT

Chinese emperors traced their ancestral lines back to dragons and claimed the benign, all-powerful creatures as their own personal emblems. You, too, will feel regal in this traditional robe richly patterned with five-clawed imperial dragons reaching for the "pearl" that is the source of their power. One size fits most. 100% silk. 62 in (157 cm) long.

DRAGON HILL

You can have a Dragon Hill in your own living room. A highly detailed golden dragon with four legs and wings coils around the cone base of this round, glass-topped accent table. Granite-texture resin, glass top. 18 in (46 cm) high; base and top 20 in (51 cm) in diameter.

Showing Your Dragon

Few experiences that you and your dragon can share will draw the two of you closer than participating in dragon shows. Competition requires both dragon raiser and dragon to work together for months to match abilities and skills against other handlers and their breeds. The dragon raiser, though, needs to understand that showing requires commitment – and that showing can be addictive. What might begin as a weekend hobby could become a way of life.

Why show?

There are many other reasons for showing. Here are a few:

- **Enjoyment** Despite the hard work preparing for them, shows are a vacation, holiday, adventure – something different and exciting.
- **Pride** Up to now, you and your dragon have developed a camaraderie. Now, for the first time, the two of you are working before judges, audiences, other handlers and other dragons. Public appearance induces a higher level of mutual pride.
- **Feedback** By hearing what the judges have to say about the competitive performance of the two of you, and by comparing your dragon's appearance and abilities with others of its breed, you can effectively prepare and train your dragon for its next show.
- **A noble cause** The more the public knows about dragons in general and breeds in particular, the fewer misconceptions – and the greater understanding – they will have of the unique creatures.
- **Glory** Walking off with that trophy or first-place ribbon is an unforgettable moment – for both you and your dragon.

International Dragon Shows

Beijing, China
First week of the Chinese New Year

London, England
First week in April

Athens, Greece
Second week in August

Entering a dragon show

To enter your dragon in a competition, you must have a World Dragon Club registration form confirming your dragon's breed and other pertinent information. Then you need to learn the time and place of a show in which you can enter your breed of dragon.

Some local shows are restricted to local breeds (such as those in Tarascon, France, or Alton, Illinois, which admit only Tarasque and Piasa breeds, respectively). Prestigious international shows for all breeds are held annually. Check with the WDC and the latest issue of *Dragons Unlimited* magazine for upcoming events in which you can enter your dragon.

Apply for a participation spot at least a month before the scheduled show. A week before the event you'll receive a judging programme that includes your ring number, judge's name and the approximate time your dragon will be called for judging.

What Judges Look For

The object of a dragon show is to establish which dragons most conform to the Worldwide Dragon Club's written standard of each breed's physical characteristics, temperament and abilities. Judges declare Winners of different levels of competitions and ultimately select the show's Grand Champion. To prepare and train your dragon for a dragon show, you must first know what judges look for in the various events.

Conformation

Competition begins with Class judging. Dragons competing at Class levels are not yet Champions of record. A dragon earns the title of Champion by accumulating 15 points. (The number of available points depends on the number of dragons entered in the event.) Dragons in each Class hold a "stand" position while judges inspect them for the attributes noted at right:

Correct head form (including horns, whiskers)

Brightness of eyes

Fangs (length and sharpness)

Length and colour of breathed fire (if applicable)

Texture and sharpness of groomed claws

Points System

The exhibitor leads the dragon around the show ring for the judges' observation of motion and gait appropriate to its breed.
• Points are deducted for missing scales, dull eyes, or cracked claws.
• The winner in each Class earns points towards the title.

Obedience

Only small dragons are eligible for these events, which display an animal's response to the full range of standard commands, including "Fly!" Obedience competition titles from the lowest to the highest are:

- **CD**—Companion Dragon
- **CDX**—Companion Dragon Excellent
- **UD**—Utility Dragon

Agility

Different sets of timed agility events for small and large dragons test physical ability and speed. Small dragons negotiate a course of A-frames, bar jumps, hoops, tunnels and a seesaw. Handlers and appropriate breeds of large dragons perform dressage (riding your dragon), vaulting (gymnastics on dragon-back), driving (pulling a chariot), and flying (with handler either directing the dragon from the ground or upon the animal's back).

Colour and texture of groomed scales

Symmetry of build (head, ridged back, legs, tail and wings, if applicable)

Best of Breed

The Champions and highest-ranking Winners of each breed then compete for the Best of Breed title in each of the two size divisions.

Best in Show

From among the breeds of large dragons, the head judge selects one for the ultimate honour.

Preparing to Show

When you decide to attend your first dragon show, you might think it's a long way off. It isn't. The big day will be here before you know it.

Training

Begin training at least three months before the show, for 15 or 20 minutes every day. For all shows, practise leading your dragon around its enclosure, and teach it to stand. Drill a small dragon on standard commands and repeatedly guide it through its agility course. Riding, driving and vaulting on your large dragon will require intense and patient work, and you – as well as your dragon – must be in excellent condition.

Grooming

Polishing your dragon's scales is the most demanding and time-consuming grooming task. Depending on the size of your dragon, this can take you days or even a week or more to accomplish. Rub the scales with baby oil or Vitamin E (no greasy petroleum jelly).

Trimming your dragon's claws is also essential. The laborious task requires different tools for dragons of different sizes.

Transport

Miniatures and young juveniles can be transported to the show by car or plane. Large dragons might need to be trailer-trained. Or, if the show is some distance away, shipping your dragon by rail – or even by boat – might be necessary. Winged dragons offer another transport option. In any case, don't leave packing until the last day. Gather the dragon's food, water, grooming tools, and tack and gear well in advance.

Showtime

It's the day you and your dragon have spent months preparing for.

The show area is abuzz with excitement and activity. Dragons and handlers are everywhere, nervously feeding, grooming and exercising up to the last minute.

You know your dragon is a special creature, you are proud to have raised it, and you want others – judges, exhibitors and audience alike – to see it and recognize its qualities. Now is your chance. Be confident, and your dragon, like my Rowena, can bring home a first-place ribbon.

At ringside, check in with a steward and wait for your number to be called.

Best in Show

Following all the other events of the day is the competition everyone has looked forward to – the parading and judging of each of the Best of Breeds for the ultimate honour of Best in Show.

The crowd is hushed as the winner of each Class category is introduced and circles the show ring to its allotted place. They await the final judging, the declaration of "And the winner is . . . ," and awarding of the Best in Show!

Resources
Dragon breeders/suppliers

In spite of their popularity among dragon raisers, dragons are not sold in pet stores. They are a rare animal compared to ferrets, iguanas and tarantulas, much less dogs, cats, birds and fish. The stocking of full-grown dragons in these shops is out of the question, and even miniatures are too specialized for standard retail. To acquire a dragon you will need to contact one of the few dragon breeders worldwide. Below are their classified ads that I've collected from the industry's premier trade magazine in English, *Dragons Unlimited.*

Learn your future from our Drakons
Bred from ancient stock

Oracle Source
Odós Apóllonos, Delphi, Greece

Salamanders
Fire control and makers of asbestos
Salamander Wool, Inc
Prester John Square
Addis Ababa, Ethiopia

From Worm Hill to You
Dragons to guard your treasure
Claws & Tails, Ltd
Lambton Lane, Durham, England

Sea Dragons
Saltwater and freshwater
Friends of Nessie
Pillar Dr, Loch Ness, Scotland

MOUNTAIN DRAGONS
With crests, beards and Dragon-stones

Draconce, Ltd.
Elephant Rd,
Mumbai, India

Emperor of Scaly Creatures
Sky, sea and land dragons
Supply is limited.
The House of Five Claws
Pearl St, Beijing, China

Pride of the Festival
Full-sized, miniature and
processional Tarasques
Tarasque Village
Rue du St Martha, Tarascon en
Provence, France

**Mushussus – the Consort
of Gods**
The most gentle and dignified of
all dragons
City Gate Suppliers
Marduk Ave, Babylon

Novelty Dragons
Basilisk descendants
Cockatrice City
Erewhon

Multiheaded Monsters
For use in films, side shows

Children of Typhon
Odós Heracles, Lerna, Greece

**Have you hugged your
Piasa today?**
Scare off trespassers with this
gentle beast!
Piasa Center
Marquette Ave
Alton, Illinois, USA

New Shipment of
Best-selling Dragons

*Standard Western
Dragons, both full-sized
and miniature*

Dragon House, Inc
Herald Court
Anglesey, Wales,
UK

For Your Dragon Library

I recommend that to successfully raise and care for a dragon, you gather abundant information about raising dragons and learn all you can about the lore of this grand, ancient and universal creature. Since breeders began making dragons available to the public, many books on aspects of their raising and care have been published.*
As to the shelves of books and abundance of websites on dragon lore, I'm partial, of course, to the incomparable *The Historie of Serpents*, by my ancestor, Edward Topsell. Here is a short list of books that will enhance your dragon library.

Allen, Judy, and Jeanne Griffiths, *The Book of the Dragon*.

Bates, Roy, *Chinese Dragons*.

Borges, Jorge Luis, *The Book of Imaginary Beings*.

*Broud, Amy, *Dragon Hatching for Beginners*.

*Conway, Shirley, *Your Inner Dragon*.

Cooper, J. C., *Symbolic and Mythological Animals*.

Dickinson, Peter, *The Flight of Dragons*.

*Eoff, Rod, *Basic Dragon Riding Techniques*.

*Farmer, Gladys, *Secrets of Dragon Nutrition and Feeding*.

Gould, Charles, *Mythical Monsters*.

Graves, Robert, *The Greek Myths*.

*Guest, Eugene, *Showing Your Dragon: Everything You Need to Know*.

Hargreaves, Joyce, *Hargreaves New Illustrated Bestiary*.

Hoult, Janet, *Dragons: Their History & Symbolism*.

Huxley, Francis, *The Dragon: Nature of Spirit, Spirit of Nature*.

Ingersoll, Ernest, *Dragons and Dragon Lore*.

Jones, David E., *An Instinct for Dragons.*

*Levy, Christopher, *A Beginner's Guide to Showing Your Dragon.*

Nesbit, E., *The Book of Dragons.*

Nigg, Joseph, *The Book of Dragons and Other Mythical Beasts.*

Payne, Ann, *Medieval Beasts.*

*Peel, John W., *The Power of Positive Dragon Training.*

Quinn, Amanda and Donna. **Sommerland.org** (website).

Rose, Carol, *Giants, Monsters and Dragons.*

*Sassoon, J. E., *The All-Breed Dragon Grooming Guide.*

*Selle, Georges, *The Illustrated Guide to Dragon Tack and Saddlery.*

Shuker, Dr Karl, *Dragons: A Natural History.*

Smith, G. Elliot, *The Evolution of the Dragon.*

South, Malcolm, ed., *Mythical and Fabulous Creatures: A Sourcebook and Research Guide.*

*Sprache, Gretchen, *Learning Dragon Language: Intuitive Communication with a Unique Animal.*

Topsell, Edward, *The Historie of Serpents.*

Trainor, Edmund, *The Complete Dragon Training Manual.*

*Trucco, Evelina, *The Ultimate Dragon Tricks Book.*

White, T. H., *The Book of Beasts.*

*Wilbur, "Bud", *Dragon Enclosure Construction.*

* Available through *Dragons Unlimited* magazine.

Index

Credits

Dedication

For Esther, who didn't type, but who did everything else – from offering ideas and unlimited support to editing – to make this a better book than it would have been without her. **(J.N.)**

Acknowledgments (J.N.)

Page 13: Edward Topsell's Dragons from *The Historie of Serpents*.
Page 38: Father Marquette's description of the Piasa – quoted in G. Elliot Smith's *The Evolution of the Dragon*.
Page 47: Jim Nelson – edited and quoted text in "Dragon Fire".
Page 101: Esther Muzzillo – transcription of "Dragon, My Darlin'".
I would also like to thank my editor, Karen Koll, art editor, Natasha Montgomery, original text and art editors Susie May and Anna Knight, and the following for their various contributions to this book: Marjorie Muzzillo, Jim Nelson, Gary Reilly, Oliver Monk, Lawrence Dunning, Joseph Hutchison, Amanda Quinn, Kayla Pacheco, and Joey, Jill, Jessie, Jayce, Cassidy and Max.

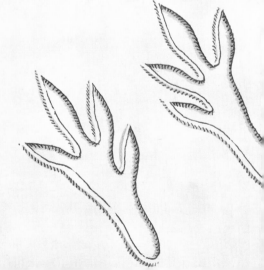